Your DATA is F*CKED

FOR MARKETERS

MARK MCKENZIE

YOUR DATA IS F**KED
– FOR MARKETERS

Your data is F**ked. Here is why and how to fix it.

Your data, reports, insights, and dashboards are totally F**ked. At least, it feels that way. You are not alone. Many other marketers are in your boat.

Good data = better marketing. We all get that, but by knowing our customers, we can offer more personalised communication and have better conversations. We can understand what is working in our campaigns and what isn't. With automation, communication can be scaled, highly effective, and highly profitable. With AI, it can be turbocharged, and with the right models, we can confidently predict the future.

Customers want and expect you to know them, but they also don't want to be stalked, spammed, chased, cajoled, and generally bothered without permission or reward for their attention.

The frameworks, exercises, and strategies in this book are designed for you to go back to time and time again; the concepts are easy enough to follow for anyone new to this increasingly critical and once specialist-only area.

This is a book for the frustrated, dazed, and confused containing everything you need to know as a marketer or decision maker to hold your own and to understand why your data is F**ked and how to fix it.

This is a book for digital marketers of all creeds, but if a family member or friend has casually and repeatedly assumed that you 'do SEO' – and you don't – this is probably the book for you.

The issue of F**ked data is persistent because it is a symptom of a much deeper set of challenges. Let's start by understanding the problem. Go get a coffee and pull up a chair.

INTRODUCTION

When I first had the idea for this book, I thought about writing a textbook; I wanted something I could use to file and organise everything I've read, learnt, debated, and processed and could pull out whenever I got stuck or needed a reference point to go to back to. I got excited about that idea for about a day before the thought of writing a textbook moved me to boredom and the thought of all that work that nobody would read to tears. So, I thought, literally, fuck it, I'll try and write something on digital analytics and digital growth that a busy marketing manager or consultant might actually read, and Your Data Is F**ked was born. I hope you enjoy reading this as much as I enjoyed writing it.

My journey into web analytics was born from frustration – the same frustration that I believe still drives marketers today: how do I prove to [CLIENT or SENIOR STAKEHOLDER] that [CAMPAIGN, WEBSITE, APP, LANDING PAGE] is working? The question should be, how do I know IF it's working? Most of the time, people just wanted proof of what they already knew, not for new information or insights but for proof that X caused Y, whether it did or not.

After looking for the data in the standard web analytics tool Google Analytics, I realised that, yes, my data is F**ked, because my tracking is F**ked. This then brought me and most marketers to the next problem, talking to the uninterested technical expert or gatekeeper. Your web or app developer might be a lovely or brilliant person, but nine times out of ten, they have yet to develop an interest in data or tracking. They're busy, and your request is an inconvenience.

My personal development in web analytics came from an immediate interest and a natural sense of bullshit. Most of the time I reached out for help, I would get responses lacking logic, often being told that some type of tracking could not be done. It became my self-assumed role to show not just the value of the campaigns but the value of good data and good tracking and then work out how to achieve that by working across the differences and misunderstandings between brands, marketers, and developers.

Fast forward, and the general knowledge, skills, and attitudes around data analytics and its importance have greatly improved, moving from 'is that to do with SEO?' to a must-have in a relatively short time, massively expedited by one pandemic and a global overnight paradigm shift to digital-first – but the challenge has also got much more complex and confusing. The foundation of previously free and easily accessible, usable customer data is unstable and being eroded more with every anti-tracking browser update; but, seemingly paradoxically, at the same time, customers also expect greater levels of personalisation and informed communication for us to know what they want.

There is no quick fix. To solve this problem, brands are looking at various tools, technologies, and tactics, and stakeholders and marketers trust them to make those decisions in silos, without good strategic oversight. The solution to this is broader and affects all departments (not just marketing and IT); it requires informed strategic leadership from the top down.

This book will take you through that journey, through the Analytics Maturity Curve and the processes, plans, people, and decisions we'll need to make to get there. We'll look at pillars to success, explore the exciting opportunities possible with this new permission-led and cooperative way of working, and finally understand why Your Data is F**ked and what to do about it.

The issue of F**ked data is persistent because it is a symptom of a much deeper set of challenges. Let's start by understanding the problem.

For Andrew Gill. So long, and thanks for all the fish.

CONTENTS

YOUR DATA IS F**KED – FOR MARKETERS

Introduction

Dedication

PART ONE – UNDERSTANDING THE PROBLEM	1
Chapter 1 – Climbing the Analytics Maturity Curve	4
1.1 – A Path to Somewhere	5
1.2 – Looking Forward to Good Data	10
Chapter 2 – Foundation Achieved	18
2.1 – Levelling-Up	19
2.2 – Crossing 'The GAP'	23
Chapter 3 – The Power of One	35
3.1 – The Forgotten Role of the 'Marketer'	36
3.2 – Let's (First-PARTY) Data.	42
Chapter 4 – Surviving the Cookie Apocalypse	49
4.1 – Cookie Monster Forever	50
4.2 – Solutions and Possible Data Strategies	59
Chapter 5 – The Pillars of Personalisation	63
5.1 – The Parthenon to Sustainable Growth	64
5.2 – Analytics Maturity as an Organisation	70
5.3 – Data as a Resource	74
5.4 – Tools and Tech	79

PART TWO – TAKING ACTION	85
Chapter 6 – Plan, Plan, Plan	88
6.1 – Plan or Plan to Fail	89
6.2 – Project Plan – The Unwritten	90
6.3 – Solution Designs – Birdseye View	99
6.4 – Measurement Plans – The Missing	102
6.5 – Code, Metrics, and Dimension Libraries	106
Chapter 7 – Picking a Strategy	111
7.1 – It Comes from the Top – or Not	112
7.2 – Opportunity COST	116
7.3 – Risk	117
7.4 – The Wheel of Growth	123
7.5 – Personalisation Strategy and Process	127
Chapter 8 – Let's Go Tool Shopping	134
8.1 – The Pitch	135
8.2 – Off-the-Shelf or Off-Track	139
8.3 – Data Sovereignty	145
8.4 – Real Cost	148
8.5 – Considerations per Tool	153
Chapter 9 – Reporting vs. Dashboarding	159
9.1 – Who Wants Data	160
9.2 – Leveraging the DIKW Pyramid	162
9.3 – Apples to Apples	166
9.4 – The Perfect Self-Service Dashboard	171
Chapter 10 – Who Is Missing?	181
10.1 – Who Does What?	182
10.2 – The Two Tracks	186
10.3 – The Divide	191

PART THREE – WHERE DO WE GO FROM HERE?	199
Chapter 11 – Times Are a-Changin'	201
11.1 – Predictions and Reflections	202
11.2 – Prediction 1 – Winners and Losers	204
11.3 – Prediction 2 – Track 2 Has More Distance	206
11.4 – Prediction 3 – Anticipation Becomes Real	210
11.5 – Prediction 4 – More Money for Lawyers	215
11.6 – Prediction 5 – Tech Wreck Refocus	218
Chapter 12 – Conclusion	224
12.1 – The Rinse and Repeat of F**ked Data	225
Glossary	234
Additional Resources	244
About The Author	253

PART ONE – UNDERSTANDING THE PROBLEM

If you are reading this, I assume you have purchased this book. You've flicked through randomly, glanced at the cover, and skimmed the main introduction. Let's kick things off, shall we?

Part One is about understanding the problem; to do that, we need some memorable frameworks, examples, and shared foundational knowledge. This allows us to enter the room and know roughly where all the doors, windows, and corners are before we rush straight over to the steaming pile of shit on the carpet. It gives us context and perspective.

The information contained has not all been created by myself;

I'm part of a broader field and industry. Some material is presented as is, and some is adapted and repurposed from other sources. In those cases, I have strived to give the original creator fair credit and personally sought permission to use their material.

I can promise you that I have spent a long time, nearly a decade, sourcing, understanding, absorbing, and regurgitating this stuff in a critical environment where the end user is a marketer just like yourself expecting professional advice and sound, no-nonsense support and direction.

We'll familiarise ourselves with **The Analytics Maturity Curve**; there are many like it, but this is mine. We will break down the various levels and assess where you are on the curve. We'll work through level 1 to level 5 and look at each level's most critical steps and pitfalls, stopping to highlight **The GAP**, what it is, and how we cross it.

We'll take our learnings from Kmart, Wickes, Mint.com, and the recent Cannes Lions winner, Data Tienda.

With sound foundations under our feet, we'll take a good step back again and honestly review our role as marketers and the challenge of being pulled in so many different directions. We'll consider what we're trying to achieve for our clients, bosses, and customers and bring it down to The **Power of One**.

Once we're armed with some of these ideas, approaches, and frameworks, we'll detail the difference between first- and third-party data, how it's linked to the coming **Cookie Apocalypse**, and why everything we do as digital marketers is about to be pulled away underneath us. Out of the rubble, we will create new approaches and revisit the old first-party and server-side data collection methods we should have pursued in the first place.

I'll balance the technical know-how with strategy so you can have an informed conversation with your developer about your data strategy and how best to move forward.

When we're all caught up and understand why our data is F**ked, we're ready to start taking action. To do this, we'll look at the **Pillars of Personalisation**, data as a resource, analytics maturity, and our tools, and work through an approach that will help us to explore the exciting opportunities possible with this new permission-led and cooperative way of working.

CHAPTER 1 – CLIMBING THE ANALYTICS MATURITY CURVE

In this chapter, I'll introduce you to one of the most essential frameworks in this book – the Analytics Maturity Curve. Although relatively simple, it has the power to orientate us at every level of our journey. We can agree on where we are now, where we want to be, and how determined we are to get there, but why bother? Do we just want unF**ked data, or will we do something more impressive?

We'll go through level 1 and what it means to be looking forward to good data and why bad data is such a prevalent problem. We'll look at the importance of an objective audit. I'll give you the must-have information you should consider for any audit or reconciliation, starting with the new Google Analytics 4 as our example and what you should expect from any new implementation or audit.

1.1 – A PATH TO SOMEWHERE

In this book, you will find many frameworks, images, diagrams, glossaries, and workable templates to take into your role. I'll present you with questions to consider in each chapter to bring this all back to your own uniquely F**ked situation so you can finally understand why your data is F**ked and what to do about it. Let's start with one of the most essential and valuable frameworks.

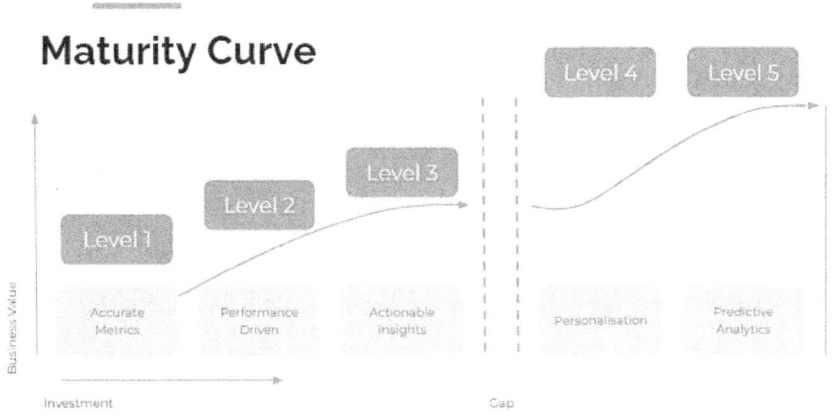

Source: McKtui Consulting

There are many like it, but this one is mine. It is my life. I must master it as I must master my life. Without it, my analysis would be useless. Full Metal Jacket – probably, if the war was about data.

There are lots of marketing curves out there, typically to explain the various stages of development. My favourite was Bill Gassman's 'Tool Maturity'. It was this model and conversations with clients and colleagues that led to the 'Analytics Maturity Curve' stages that every company could go through to achieve whatever outcome they set their sights on.

Our graph shows us time and expected investment going from left to right, starting from level 1, eventuating at level 5. The real value to the business increases as we make our way through, and the curve bends up gradually before leaping up from level 3 to level 4 and then to level 5. Between level 3 and level 4, there is an obvious GAP, but don't worry about that yet; let's walk before we run and look at the reasons for this later.

So how mature is your organisation in digital and web analytics and why does that matter, and how do we make sure we don't keep falling off?

'Maturity describes how deeply and effectively your organisation uses tools, people, processes, and strategy to manage and analyses data to inform business decisions.' - Król, Karol and Zdonek, Dariusz. "Analytics Maturity Models: An Overview."

Most importantly, it's a great place to begin and define our problem. Your company may not know a lot about analytics. Still, given a simple description of each stage, most people will immediately have an opinion on where they think the company is and where they feel they should be, and that conversation is a great place to start.

The stages break down like this and are not necessarily always sequential:

Level Zero – just starting, or you do not trust your data. You may have some version of Google Analytics (GA) added to your website, or you're using a Content Management System (CMS) analytics package, but you don't really understand what you're looking at, why it matters, or whether it's even accurate.

Level One – is about ensuring you have a basic level of accurate web metric reporting. You have set the foundations for actionable insights with reliable basic web metrics. You have limited marketing and single-source web data but trust its accuracy. You've got – <u>Basic, Accurate Web Metrics.</u>

Level Two – is about using your data to act and continuing to work on metrics, accuracy, and process. You are optimising behaviour and traffic based on known previously-agreed key performance indicators (KPIs) and agreed targets using basic self-service dashboards or custom-built reports. You are doing – <u>Performance Driven Marketing.</u>

Level Three – is about laying the groundwork for greater personalisation and uncovering detailed insights and wisdom. You have established vital and detailed target segments and specific user journeys. You are starting to integrate more sources of customer data. You're building your way to – <u>Actionable Insights.</u>

Level Four – is about personalisation and taking a 330° view of a customer (30° because of privacy). You have built models on Customer Lifetime Value (CLV) and are automating either content or marketing. You likely have a Customer Relationship Management (CRM) system integrated with the rest of your marketing business technology stack. You may use a Customer Data Platform (CDP) and an integrated data warehouse. There are various degrees to success, but holy shit, you're doing it – <u>Omni-channel Marketing through Automated Personalisation.</u>

Level Five – is taking the foundation of all the work completed and applying data science-powered analysis (often with artificial intelligence (AI)), and implementation over the top. You are planning to use or are already using AI and move from 'Descriptive' to 'Predictive' and 'Prescriptive' analytics. Hello, great sage; you're using <u>Predictive Analytics.</u>

The first questions to ask regarding your organisation are:

- What level would you say you are now?

- What level do you hope to be in the next six months?
- What level do you hope to be in the next 12 months?
- What level do you hope to be eventually?

Knowing where you are and where you want to be is not only the start of the conversation but will help you to start assessing how much investment and time may be required to get there. Just getting some level of agreement around where you are and where you want to be is step one. For some companies, if you are small, or can't readily see the possible benefits for you, then stages 1–2 may be good enough; but make sure you at least ask the question because if your competitors or customers decide it's not, you might be in for some trouble.

We will go through the details of each stage, but here is an example of what could feature in a possible project plan for your organisation. This example is for a medium- to corporate-sized business. Throughout the book, where we don't have an appropriate real-life example, we'll use an up-and-coming, ready-to-take-industry-by-storm and entirely imaginary business: Shoe-in.com.

The Analytics Maturity Curve – Example

Following our overall strategic priorities and project goal, we are working to enable Shoe-in.com to progress from level 1 (as assessed) to level 3 in 12 months through the Analytics Maturity Curve led by the following key activities. This is how they relate to each stage:

Level 1–3 activities (looking back):

- Establish Technical Foundations – Implement a CDP to standardise existing data collection and serve as a foundation for later Level 4–5 activities, such as CRM integration and predictive analytics. The initial focus will be Web Analytics tools.

- Implementation of Core Web Analytics – Key groundwork completed regarding existing solution design, basic tracking of page views, events, and measurement planning. More testing is also recommended to validate existing tracking.
- Self-Service Dashboards; Tactical and Strategic Reporting – Empowering the team at Shoe-in.com to self-serve and focus on business decision-making with up-to-date data and insights at their fingertips.
- Segmentation and User Journey Mapping – There are gaps in coverage of engagement tracking for all assets/value streams. Work must be done to ensure that personas or segments are set up correctly and usable across all current and future sources and destinations.

Level 4–5 activities:

- Data Integration (chasm) – Current priority. Integration of other existing MarTech tools, such as CRM.
- Data Science and Performance Management (looking forward) – Development of further personalisation and statistical analysis-driven segmentation such as propensity to covert (high engagement). Plan to review database connections.

A list like this, although requiring much more detail in practice, allows us to plan and prioritise the next steps, mapping our trajectory through the Analytics Maturity Curve, preparing for potential difficulties, and identifying lack of knowledge in certain areas.

1.2 – LOOKING FORWARD TO GOOD DATA

Before we can start looking forward, both in terms of making valuable predictions about the future and finally overcoming our F**ked data, we need to assess and build our foundations.

Steps 1–4 are all about looking back: we're seeking to understand what has happened and what is happening. The stages build in complexity before reaching the most challenging and testing stage, Level 4 – The GAP. Crossing the GAP requires talking to other silos and getting other people onside and aligned with our vision, and to do that, we need the God-given mandate from senior leadership to do so. This is where we have to move past just relying on our CRM or GA and look to centralise the collection and distribution of data across many different tools and departments. Don't fear. You should not tackle this all at once but start small. Let's start looking forward to good reliable data.

Level One – Just Starting, Or You Do Not Trust Your Data.

Only 54% of marketing decisions are being influenced by marketing analytics, according to Gartner's latest Marketing

Data and Analytics Survey 2020.

This is a worrying trend when respondents cite poor data quality, unactionable results, and nebulous recommendations as top reasons they don't rely on analytics to make decisions.

Although we may have completed some of the tasks at other levels, by all likelihood, if you picked up this book, you're starting somewhere around here. At some point, your organisation could have been flying at level 3 with the wind in its hair. Still, now you are sub-zero because some combination of mismanagement and misunderstanding has led your organisation's analytics to fall off by the wayside, or perhaps some technological change has forced you back to the point of outdated and unreliable data.

When writing this book, a recent research piece said that 'Google Analytics is used by 28.1 million websites, and approximately 55.49% of all websites use Google Analytics.' Universal Analytics (3) was released in 2012, and since then, millions of us marketers have got used to its structure and interface. By July 1, 2023, all those users must have transitioned to the new and very different Google Analytics 4.

Huge, unwieldy legacy implementations used by multiple people and marketers and customised by numerous developers over many years will need to be quickly and correctly transitioned. On top of this, it will take time for us marketers and analysts to get our heads around this new tool. It's a tremendous upheaval and, for many companies, a forced fall off and tumble down the Analytics Maturity Curve.

The marketers struggling most with these changes have no plan to work from or no records of how, why, and when something was implemented. To get from 0 to 1, we need a few things in place.

Initial Audits And Reconciliation

First, a tirade... Whatever you do, don't tell me, 'It's working'. This is the worst thing you can say. If you hear anyone say it's working, the hair on your neck should stand up, and you should come out with chills. When I hear the completely lacking and sketchy words, I breathe and ask what <u>exactly</u> is working, by how much, and show me the proof. The further away from the data that the person you are working with is, the more you shouldn't take this answer at face value and let your bullshit indicator start firing; often, it just means 'I added the code following a blog, and I saw myself appear in real-time in the GA interface.'

A good structure for an audit is:

1. Code
2. Configuration
3. Data Integrity

Checking the code is simple and most often completed correctly. You can also do this yourself to some level, and I recommend having a debugger like Google Debugger on your browser if you're using GA.

As for configuration, they or you should be asking questions about how you would like your analytics configurated. Some settings have increasingly important legal ramifications and must be checked with you first, or is your agency or web company blindly ticking 'OK' without reviewing your data policy? Probably at this point, you may be thinking 'Oh shit, do we need a data policy?' Unfortunately, yes, but even something simple could do for now.

GA4 Configuration
Account, Property and Data Stream Settings

Section		Title	Settings/notes	
Account Section				
	Account Settings			
		Account Name	Shoe-in.com	Done
		Account Id	2345677	Done
		Country of Business	UK	Done
		Data Sharing Settings	On as requested	Done
	Account access management			
		Check Account Access (if required)	Require more information	FALSE
	All Filters			
		Check Filters at account level	All standard filters applied	Done
	Account Change History			
		Check change history (if required)	Checked, nothing unusual	Done
Property Section				
	Setup Assistant			
		Data Collection	Standard	Done
		Property Settings	Checked, nothing unusual	Done

Source: McKtui Consulting

Data Collection Legal Considerations

Again, using GA as an example and with my disclaimer here.

The following does not constitute legal advice. During the setup, there are several terms and conditions that Google will ask the implementer to agree to on your behalf – depending on the functionality of the setup; these are as follows:

Google Ads Data Processing Terms* –

- *https://business.safety.google/adsprocessorterms/*
- Google Analytics Terms of Service Agreement *–https://marketingplatform.google.com/about/analytics/terms/us/*
- Google Measurement Controller-Controller Data Protection Terms *–https://support.google.com/analytics/answer/9024351?hl=en*

Here is the data typically collected by GA4:

The following link has the key 'Dimensions and Metrics' listed as part of the installation:

- *https://support.google.com/analytics/answer/9143382?*

*hl=en#zippy=%2Csession%2Cuser%2Cuser-lifetime
%2Cpage-screen%2Cevent%2Cgeneral
%2Cdemographics%2Cattribution*

Google generally strives to ensure that personally identifiable information (PII) is not collected, but the definition of what constitutes PII changes market-to-market. Occasionally PII can be collected accidentally in URLs.

Finally, they are either auditing your existing implementation or completing a new implementation. In the latter case, you should expect some communication around benchmark numbers to confirm if your setup is genuinely working. Some larger organisations perform a regression test on larger setups to see if there is a significant tracking difference in large transitions from one tool to another or some other data source. However, even for small setups, it makes sense just eyeballing and screenshotting critical metrics over time. This is really important and often missed.

Universal Analytics or GA3 often had issues with Bounce Rate, and this regularly pointed to a more significant problem. One of those issues could be double code. If your team had not caught the common issue of adding code twice, you could often catch the issue in a Data Integrity Check, where we could check the 'continuity' of key metrics either 3 days, 1 week, 1 month, or even 12 months after implementation.

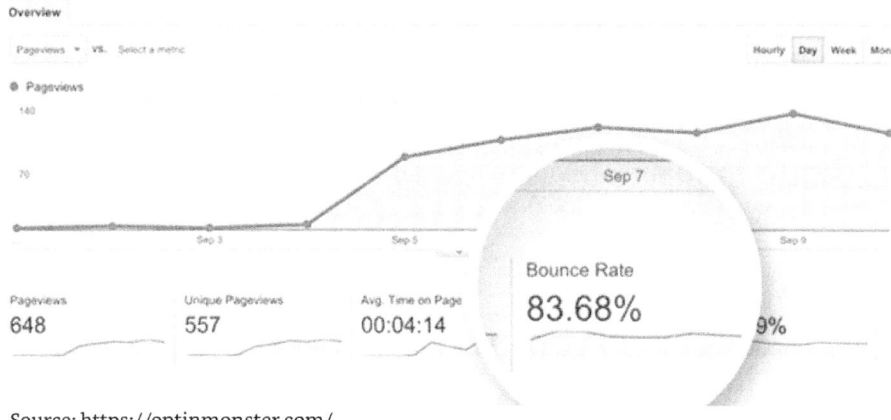

Source: https://optinmonster.com/

In this case, the Bounce Rate drops to effectively zero because a hit is counted twice in quick succession, so actually, the User in Session cannot bounce away from the page because the second false hit is taken as some kind of interaction that did not happen. The chart above shows how the situation can be murky as this double code may only be on some sections of the website, making the drop look more normal as it's averaged across the simultaneously 'working' and 'not working' tracking.

Another important step is creating and maintaining a measurement plan (Chapter 4 Plan, Plan, Plan). If you want good data, you must have a measurement plan freely shared and understood throughout your organisation. Typically, the best tool for this is a shareable spreadsheet using SharePoint or Google Sheets. This is so important that we devote an entire chapter to it later in the book.

Your initial setup should begin modestly: start with the must-haves and build as your skills, requirements, and resources do, but everything on your app or web page that you are looking to track now and in the future should be entered into your measurement plan.

Once we have completed a basic setup, tested our setup, and been careful to follow our measurement plan, we can move on to using our data to inform decisions, and because we've been involved in or led the initial steps, we can trust that our foundation web analytics data is correct. We've got a good idea of what we're tracking and why, so we can start pulling this data into dashboards and reports depending on whom the audience is, which will determine what data we pull.

After this chapter, you should understand the **Analytics Maturity Curve** and its different levels. You will know where you are on the curve and where you want to be.

You will be familiar with structured approaches to auditing tools like Google Analytics, looking at Code, Configuration, and Data Integrity. You will start to consider your own data policy and what a disclaimer could look like.

We're ready to look at the rest of the Analytics Maturity Curve in more detail, starting with Section 2.1 – **Levelling-Up**.

References And Bibliography

1. Business Dit. (n.d.). 50+ Google Analytics Statistics That Matter in 2021. Retrieved from https://www.businessdit.com/google-analytics-statistics/
2. Cannes Lions. (n.d.). Creative Data Lions. Retrieved from https://www.canneslions.com/awards/lions/creative-data
3. IBM. (n.d.). Predictive Analytics. Retrieved from https://www.ibm.com/topics/predictive-analytics#:~:text=Predictive%20analytics%20is%20a%20branch,to%20identify%20risks%20and%20opportunities.
4. Predictive Analytics World. (2021, April 26). The Death of Big Data and the Emergence of the Multi-Cloud Era. Retrieved from https://

www.predictiveanalyticsworld.com/machinelearningtimes/the-death-of-big-data-and-the-emergence-of-the-multi-cloud-era/10527/#:~:text=Big%20Data%20is%20now%20a,and%20subsequent%20market%20capitalization%20drop.
5. Hawke Media. (n.d.). Predictive Analytics in Marketing: A Comprehensive Guide. Retrieved from https://hawke.ai/blog/predictive-analytics-in-marketing/
6. Karunasekara, C., & Perera, G. (2021). The role of analytics maturity in digital transformation. *Information*, 11(3): 142. doi: 10.3390/info11030142

CHAPTER 2 – FOUNDATION ACHIEVED

In this chapter, we explore the levels of analytics maturity from level 1 to level 5.

Discover level 2, where data drives action, and learn how to develop metrics and streamline processes. Dive into level 3, where the groundwork for personalisation is laid. Cross 'The GAP' to reach level 4 and better understand customers using real-world examples.

Finally, explore the possibilities of predictive analytics and its attainability. We uncover the challenges and rewards of each Analytics Maturity Curve level and lay the foundation for success.

2.1 – LEVELLING-UP

Level 2 – Using Our Data To Drive Actions And Continuing To Work On Metrics, Accuracy, And Process

To move into levels 2 and 3, we'll be looking to work through several vital tasks depending on how large our organisation is and how far up the curve we're ultimately looking to go. Those tasks often centre around reporting, dashboarding, and further planning for additional tracking and more detailed insights and questions.

When approaching reporting and dashboarding, it's important not to rush in (Chapter 9 – Reporting vs. Dashboarding). Much time is spent building reports and dashboards for stakeholders who do not value or understand them. This is also the most visible part of what you're offering and so most susceptible to HIPPO bias and 'helpful' opinions.

HIPPO is an acronym representing the common factors that can influence decision-making: the opinions of the highest-paid person, individual experience or intuition, personal biases, politics, and organisational culture.

Just as we want to include our key stakeholders in the right stages of the Measurement Plan, we need to ensure our end users are aligned with how the data you prepare will look and should be used. If you don't do this, they may think your data is F**ked, even if it's not. Just one doubtful and unanswered question or comment from the C-suite or senior leadership team can send your report up in flames, with doubts cast on the rest of the data's accuracy and, therefore, all your insights being called into question. It is better to keep them in the fold and onside as you work through a proper reporting structure and strategy and provide wireframes of possible dashboards and key metrics before catching them off guard with a dazzling data puke that creates more questions than it answers. Data puke is term coined wonderfully by author Avinash Kaushik.

Level 3 – Laying The Groundwork For Greater Personalisation, And Uncovering Detailed Insights And Wisdom

In level 3, it is important to understand what you are doing and why you are doing it. Your detailed reporting provides great insights using tactical and strategic reporting to the right level within your organisation. Now you're starting to look outside your silo and area and looking to start designing solutions around how to track and service your customers across multiple channels and touchpoints (Chapter 3 – The Power of One). You're having conversations about customer relationship management (CRM) systems and exciting new tools (Chapter 8 – Let's Go Tool Shopping) and about whether we get a new content management system (CMS) or how to integrate our existing tools and technology better. You may have other marketing tools, such as email-based or programmatic, running alongside your paid search or facebook ads, and you want to join those audiences. Perhaps you have lots of great offline data completely isolated from you, your own data, and your team.

You will then go beyond the standard metrics and dimensions and start building your own scoring or indicators. A user experience team may look to introduce page or customer quality scoring like Google's HEART Metrics.

HEART Framework

	Goals	Signals	Metrics
Happiness			
Engagement			
Adoption			
Retention			
Task Success			

Source: McKtui Consulting based on Google's HEART Framework.

To better surface real information about on-site behaviour or build out your own customer lifetime value equation, understanding the value of the sale is more than just that one sale; it's every other product they go on to buy and the additional customers they bring along with them.

If your website is heavy on content and you want your visitors to spend a long time there, a content stickiness score could be much more helpful than page time or bounce rate: adding a compounding value for every additional piece of content a user ingests after an initial piece or landing page.

You're making the best of understanding and perfecting the few silos of data you have access to right now, but this is where we take the leap of faith, rally our expeditionary force and cross 'The GAP'; the rewards are high, but so could be the costs (Chapter 7 – Picking a Strategy). How do we ensure we have the proper business case to make this decision, and what do we need to know? First, we need to know if we have what it takes because we may need to build in those areas or outsource (Chapter 5 – The Pillars of Personalisation), and then we need a plan (Chapter 6 – Plan, Plan, Plan).

Hopefully, you're starting to feel there may be some method to this madness by now.

2.2 – CROSSING 'THE GAP'

Before we look to cross 'The GAP', let's revisit the definition of level 4:

Level 4 – is about personalisation and taking a 330° view of a customer (330° because of privacy). You have built models on customer lifetime value (CLV) and are automating either content or marketing. You likely have a customer relationship management system (CRM) integrated with the rest of your marketing business technology stack. You may use a customer data platform (CDP) and an integrated data warehouse. There are various degrees to success but holy shit, you're doing it – <u>Omni-channel Marketing through Automated Personalisation.</u>

Crossing 'The GAP' is difficult because you suddenly need to look beyond the marketing team and often the marketing budget. You will need to work more closely with developers and IT, potentially bring on costly tools and contractors, and get some solid senior stakeholder support. It's a tall order, but something you can chip away at. Let's look at examples and case studies of how other companies have taken this leap of faith.

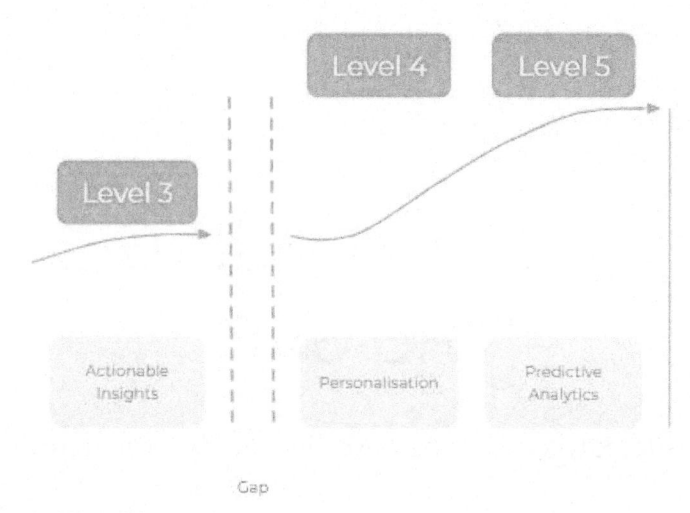

Source: McKTui Consulting.

Level 4 – Building A Better Picture – Data Tienda

Let's look at what can be achieved with a recent Cannes Awards winner. First, if you don't know of Cannes, it's an award ceremony often beyond reproach with little room to influence or buy awards.

Millions of low-income women in Mexico cannot become entrepreneurs because they cannot access bank credit. According to the National Banking and Securities Commission, 83% don't have a 'credit history', so their loan applications are rejected. Paradoxically, they are women who have received loans from neighbourhood stores all their lives, so they actually have a long credit history. Data Tienda collects this information from the neighbourhood businesses and uses it to create a digital credit history that secures them with the banks and allows them to obtain microcredits, financial inclusion, and economic autonomy.'

Data Tienda was described as, 'A powerful example of elevating "invisible data"'. It was brought to the competition by investment firm WeCapital in partnership with DDB México and centred around *raising awareness about the challenges women in Mexico face when trying to take out loans that require a credit score. The campaign, 'Data Tienda', earned the Grand Prix award; it populated legacy pen-and-paper bookkeeping data from local bodegas into a database that created a credit score 86% of Mexican women didn't have. This credit score then allowed the bank to give them small business loans.*

This is a good reminder when evaluating our data resources (Chapter 5 – The Pillars of Personalisation) to think creatively about what we have that could be used and unique to our organisation and to consider this even if we don't currently have access to that data or know we could get it.

In this example, the project used a form of simple AI to collect the data they needed, whereas in the past, collecting the required data would likely have been cost-prohibitive. Rather than rely on a large team of data collectors, they created WhatsApp bots to deliver the form to the nearly 50,000 shopkeepers that had participated as of the time of the case study. And it worked! Over 10,000 new credit records were generated, allowing participants to move forward within modern banking practices.

An excellent place to start is by bringing our existing data together for an immediate problem or application and asking the initial question, should we have this data at all? How can we automate a process that enables our customers to opt in and out freely without resentment, and what can we offer in return for this data?

This is often referred to as the value exchange. With our Cannes example, it's a win-win for most involved: customers share data to get loans, and those providing the loans get to issue more loans and improve overall credit scores, which ensures a high likelihood that loans won't default.

It can be as simple as improving a customer's experience with the brand by not advertising 'at them' with messages that are not relevant – as long as the data you're asking for is not too personal or time-consuming for the customer to provide.

Imagine this at your local market; this is what we frequently do online.

Hey Mr 'iNsErT cUsToMer NaMe', I saw you looking at bananas (the customer has just bought a banana). Would you like some bananas with your purchase? You seem like the kind of persona that likes bananas, unknown male, age 24–30. The market stall owner then proceeds to email the customer about bananas, even though they have only just bought bananas and won't need more bananas for a few weeks.

For obvious reasons, the customer politely asks not to be contacted again about bananas by opting out of an email campaign (which is often now also, for obvious reasons, a legal requirement). The market stall owner proceeds to follow the now ex-customer around with a large banner that says, 'Hey, do you like bananas?' – following them into social situations or while they are booking flights. It doesn't matter, just wherever and whenever the market stall owner can fit his big banana sign.

The customer finally runs out of bananas and actually does like the market stall owner's bananas, but he now comes back to the market stall with a large Harry Potter-style incognito cloak in the hope of being able to buy some bananas in peace.

This would be insane in the real world, so why do we continue to do it online? It's because, at scale, it can work enough of the time to be viable. Of course, we don't experience the obvious embarrassment first-hand for all the times it doesn't work and ends up driving potential and repeat customers away.

How we extract, collect, transfer, and share this data is now often to use a specific tool called a customer data platform (CDP). The CDP acts as the connector and collector for the various data points collected at various stages by the organisation for use in various marketing tools.

To show how this can work, here is a case study from Acquia, a CDP company working with Wickes.

Acquia CDP: Wickes Boosts Shopper Engagement, Customer Support
----

Wickes, a home improvement retailer with 240 stores across the United Kingdom, had two goals in mind when they started the search for a customer data platform: reducing costs related to the outsourcing of marketing functions (such as targeting and database management) and to take control of the company's customer data, which includes both Wickes' 'DIY' and trade customers.

Hayley Clifford, Wickes' senior CRM and loyalty manager, and her team ultimately decided that the Acquia CDP could help them accomplish these goals and more. While marketing teams traditionally use customer data platforms, this was not true for Wickes. In fact, Wickes' CRM team was the primary user of the CDP for the first two years. Seeing the benefits of the CDP realised by the CRM team, the platform is now also being used by the marketing insights team, who use it to analyse customer purchase behaviour, as well as by the social media and digital teams. The ability of various teams to leverage customer data has had the effect of creating a seamless and more efficient cross-team approach to serving Wickes' customers, raising the quality of engagement both online and off.

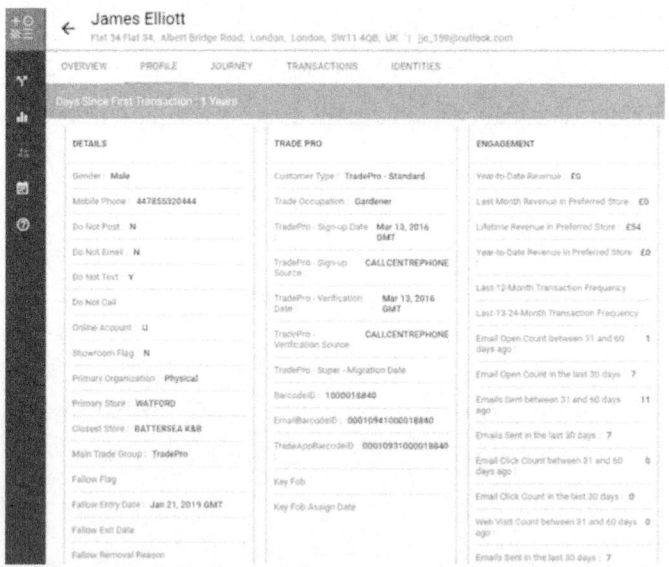

Source: CMSWIRE - 4 CDP Case Studies: Acquia, Arm Treasure Data, BlueConic, Lytics

Wickes' goals for their online retail operations included increasing customer engagement and conversion through more relevant email campaigns and decreasing cart abandonment. Before deploying the CDP, they had no way to mitigate cart abandonment. After deployment, Clifford and her team were able to:

- *Map the top 1,000 search terms to the product category*
- *Capture browsing behaviour using the AgilOne webtag*
- *Send personalised emails to customers who browsed but abandoned a site.*

The results of their new engagement and conversion strategy delivered beyond expectations:

- *108% increase in email opens*
- *116% increase in email clicks*
- *275% increase in purchases on the website.*

They also wanted to empower call centre agents. As a large omni-channel retailer, Wickes' number one goal is keeping their online and in-store (DIY and trade/business) customers happy. Call centres are a vital customer touchpoint for Wickes, generating revenue and contributing to customer satisfaction and retention. Wickes can provide more personalised customer service by using Acquia's platform to surface specific information, giving the call centre agents a complete picture of the customer, including previous support calls and transaction history, so they can personalise the call experience and resolve inquiries more quickly.

Before the Acquia CDP, agents only had visibility of purchase history and previous communication with the call centre. Agents had to ask the IT department for customer details and loyalty programme memberships. Agents now use the CDP to identify whether the customer is part of a loyalty programme. Agents tailor the phone conversation or email based on the caller's profile. Agents can now manage tickets without needing to involve IT, and there has been a 98% increase in operational efficiency.

In this practical example, we can see how navigating through and crossing 'The GAP' can be possible and the potential rewards for doing so for both our customers and us. Acquia is just one of the potential CDPs we could consider as part of our MarTech Stack and future solution designs.

Level 5 – Moving Forward With Predictive Analytics

Wow, you made it; you've surpassed 90% of the companies out there. You're up on stage and receiving rewards for innovative campaigns based on exceptional insights; that's if your company bought enough tables or seats. No correlation there.

Stage 5 is a game changer. That's when we stop looking back so much and start making predictions. Based on what we know about previous results, we can predict all types of things. How much traffic should we be getting? What the conversion rate should be? And more importantly, based on what we know about our customers, segments, or audiences – who is most likely to convert? – so that before they do so, we can adjust our bidding accordingly: bidding higher for audiences with a higher likelihood to convert, and passing on those that look like tyre-kickers.

Any tool or innovation can be used for good or bad, and it's up to us to provide that principled lens to ensure we follow ethical practices, or we risk having our new toys taken away. When explaining level 4 or 5 of the Analytics Maturity Curve, it's best to make clear that we're only ever looking to understand a 330-degree view of our customers and only that data they permit us to use.

Marketers and brands must continue to move away from the perception that data is creepy by not being creepy and using data with permission for good. As data-fuelled marketers, we can do more than sell things. We can improve things for our customers and the world.

According to IBM, predictive analytics 'is a branch of advanced analytics that predicts future outcomes using historical data combined with statistical modelling, data mining techniques, and machine learning. Companies employ predictive analytics to find patterns in this data to identify risks and opportunities. Predictive analytics is often associated with big data and data science.'

So, let's look back a little; whatever happened to big data? According to Hyoun Park, the CEO and Founder of Amalgam Insight, it died: 'The Era of Big Data passed away on June 5, 2019. The Era of Big Data is coming to an end as the focus shifts from how we collect data to processing that data in real-time. Big Data is now a business asset supporting the next eras of multi-cloud support, machine learning, and real-time analytics.

'Ultimately, it was a stepping stone to where we are now. It wasn't the answer, but it helped us ask the right questions and start thinking seriously about the data we were or could or should be gathering.

'Big Data will be remembered for its role in enabling the beginning of social media dominance, its role in fundamentally changing the mindset of enterprises in working with multiple orders of magnitude increases in data volume, and in clarifying the value of analytic data, data quality, and data governance for the ongoing valuation of data as an enterprise asset.'

So big data was an important enabler, but we quickly realised the value actually lay in our ability to manage and use that data effectively at scale. Its value is in the predictions we can make and our ability to trust the data and insights that materialise.

As we get to this stage, the learning curve ramps up again, and we'll likely need to add more specialists to our team. It all starts to seem too difficult, but it doesn't need to be, and we can start making gains bit by bit. Here is a basic model used by mint.com and market director Noah Kangan. It shows how you can create simple, effective predictions to inform your decisions.

Noah Kangan is a successful serial entrepreneur and the founder of OkDork. Before this, he was the market director for Mint.com, and he was given a seemingly unachievable target: to acquire 100,000 users in six months.

It seemed like a nearly impossible task, but rather than shrinking from the challenge, Noah leaned into it, thinking practically about where the best use of his time was – he wanted to work smart.

As with our Analytics Maturity Curve, once he had his basic data, he worked on defining the KPIs and targets that would allow him to reach his set goal – setting benchmarks and milestones for new users, sessions, and recurring revenue and breaking the goal into quarterly, monthly, and weekly targets.

Noah created a spreadsheet with this information as the third step, and it looked like this:

Source	Traffic	CTR	Conversion %	Total Users	Status	Confirmed	Confirmed Users
TechCrunch	300000	10%	25%	7500	Friend	Yes	7500
Dave McClure	30000	10%	25%	750	Friend	Yes	750
Mashable	500000	10%	25%	12500	Emailing	No	0
Reddit	25000	100%	25%	6250	Coordinated	Yes	6250
Digg	100000	100%	25%	25000	Coordinated	Yes	25000
Google Organic	5000	100%	15%	750	Receiving	Yes	750
Google Ads	1000000	3%	35%	10500	Bought	Yes	10500
Paul Stamatiou	50000	5%	50%	1250	Friend	Yes	1250
Personal Finance Sponsorships	200000	40%	65%	52000	Coordinated	Yes	52000
Okdork.com	3000	10%	75%	225	Self	Yes	225
Total Users				116725			104225

Source: Noah Kangan

As you can see, it's composed of the channels he used and goals for metrics that were important for Mint.

Noah then made a simple scoring system based on ease of implementation and potential impact. These numbers were added to create a final score, giving him the ideal combination of strategies and channels.

	A	B	C	D
1	Source	Ease of Implementation	Potential Impact	Total Score
2	PR	1	4	5
3	Influencer marketing	5	3	8
4	Target market blogs	3	5	8
5	Content marketing	4	4	8
6	Affiliate programs	2	3	5

Source: Noah Kangan

Using this simple method, he brought in 1,000,000 new users – 10 times more than the target of 100,000.

What makes this story particularly interesting is that it highlights what we mean by predictive analytics and how even the most straightforward methods can deliver or at least support the delivery of outstanding results.

In this algorithm, he uses just two constant metrics multiplied together. That's it. Noah is making the prediction himself based on his own experience. No AI is needed. The point is that you can do this, and it doesn't have to be difficult to get great results.

As we continue working through how and why our data is F**ked, we'll look at what is possible right now with predictive analytics and some key personalisation strategies that are accessible with the right mix of data, maturity, and tools.

We'll go on to look at what the future might bring, from Amazon predicting when we might want a product and stocking it before we purchase it to insurance companies using our data as consumers to assess our potential health risks and the price we pay.

◆ ◆ ◆

By now, you have gained a comprehensive understanding of the **Analytics Maturity Curve** and the essential requirements for advancing at each level. You may be thinking about how missing some levels may have contributed to your own F**ked data. You will clearly see what other organisations have achieved at each level.

Before we go further, let's take a step back and look at **The Power of One**: why we're doing this, how not to sell bananas, and what we want to achieve beyond our data being unF**ked.

References And Bibliography

1. Karunasekara, C., & Perera, G. (2021). The Role of Analytics Maturity in Digital Transformation. Information, 11(3), 142. doi: 10.3390/info1103014
2. Epsilon. (2019). Cannes Winners Showcase How Consumer Data Can Drive Powerful and Purposeful Campaigns. Retrieved from https://www.epsilon.com/us/insights/blog/cannes-winners-showcase-how-consumer-data-can-drive-powerful-and-purposeful-campaigns
3. Gratisownia. (2019). Data Tienda Wins Creative Data Grand Prix for Solving an Old Problem with a Modern Solution.

Retrieved from https://www.gratisownia.com/wpisy/data-tienda-wins-creative-data-grand-prix-for-solving-an-old-problem-with-a-modern-solution/
4. Smart Insights. (n.d.). The Digital Marketing Maturity Model. Retrieved from https://www.smartinsights.com/guides/digital-marketing-maturity-model/
5. eMarketer. (2019). The 6 Stages of Digital Marketing Maturity. Retrieved from https://www.emarketer.com/content/the-6-stages-of-digital-marketing-maturity
6. Gartner. (2020). The Digital Marketing Maturity Curve: A Framework for Measurement and Improvement [Paid content]. Retrieved from https://www.gartner.com/en/documents/3974049/the-digital-marketing-maturity-curve-a-framework-for-me
7. Karol Król and Dariusz Zdonek. (2020). "Analytics Maturity Models: An Overview." Information 11 (6): 291. https://doi.org/10.3390/info11060291
8. Adobe. (n.d.). The Digital Maturity Model: A Roadmap for Digital Transformation. Retrieved from https://www.adobe.com/content/dam/acom/en/products/adobe-experience-cloud/business-intelligence/pdfs/adobe-digital-maturity-model.pdf

CHAPTER 3 – THE POWER OF ONE

We'll examine why one-to-one conversations and personalisation are key to success in digital marketing and the underlying and unwavering marketing goal from day one.

This chapter explores the challenges of balancing customer desires for personalisation and privacy.

We examine the impact on our roles and effectiveness and why prioritising first-party data collection is crucial. Using Kmart as an example, we uncover how they collect and leverage personal data to enhance the customer experience.

We navigate this complex landscape and discover strategies to serve customers better while still respecting their privacy.

It all comes down to the **Power of One.**

3.1 – THE FORGOTTEN ROLE OF THE 'MARKETER'

Much of what we do in data and analytics and general digital marketing can seem complicated and difficult to understand or relate to. To explain the value of our offer, we must first conceptually push past the fancy titles and complicated jargon and remember what we actually do.

To do this, I use examples and frameworks we're all familiar with and bring what we're trying to achieve in a digital space back to the real world. An example I've used for years is the market stall, the grandfather of all marketing and the seed of everything we do today. That may be the first time you've connected marketing with markets.

Current data, analytics, and growth marketing are about achieving a human conversation at scale. We're trying to recreate the innate customer experience of a human talking to another human about the products we sell and the price, and offering additional incentives such as promotions to buy now. In this analogy, the place is taken care of as we're in a market. Does anyone remember the 4 P's from school?

I'm originally from the UK, and I spent a fair amount of time selling at real markets and car boot sales. My first job at ten was helping my dad cash in on the gold rush of Beanie Babies and Pokémon cards. Back then, a Charizard went for £100. Today they cost up to £1500, and old Beanie Babies aren't worth much more than a bag of flour.

If you are British, you'll be familiar with your typical cockney fruit and vegetable stallholder shouting loudly about 2 kilos of bananas for two quid (£2). They start off loud and impersonal to drive awareness and bring in customers. At the stall, they start up a conversation about the weather, but being a local, quickly jump into asking about how so-and-so is doing while adding the cheap bananas, a few extras and the weekly usual repeat purchases to the bag.

For the last ten years, I've lived in New Zealand, and this year I had a uniquely Kiwi experience in a market down the road from me. Still, for fun, I'll explain it in language and terminology we typically use online and professionally. I walked into a market unwittingly without interest in buying anything and left a pleased customer. Here is how it went. Just like our Wickes example, we'll start building a profile.

Market Stall – Selling Potted Plants For Home

Exiting Customer Attributes -

Customer status: Potential New Customer

Name: Unknown

Age: 30–40 (assumed)

Interests: Likes craft beer (wearing local Epic Brewery T-shirt)

Purchase stage: Awareness

This is how much you currently know about me in your CRM system or database, or perhaps this is stored as a segment or audience in Facebook or AdWords.

So, let's follow the interaction as I pass through the simple AIDA model.

Awareness Stage -

Seller's content - Hey, you like craft beer, aye?

My response - Yeah, Epic is my favourite.

Interest Stage -

Seller's content - Ever done any brewing? Begins to reveal a mysterious and intriguing plant.

My response - No, but I'd like to.

Content - I brew all the time. Look at this; it's an actual hop plant.

Desire Stage -

Seller's content - More interesting information about brewing with real hops and growing hop plants.

My response - Do you take cards?

It didn't take much to sell me here. I like beer, and I like mysterious beer-smelling plants. At some point, I could imagine myself as a backyard brewer.

Action Stage -

Seller's content - Buy now offer. No, I don't, but there is a cash machine around the corner, and I'll take $10 instead of $12 for easy change.

Now you know he's good. I have a reason to go now and get the money, not put it off till later and then forget.

Post Purchase -

Seller's content - I'll be here next week with different hop varieties. What's your name? Here's my card. The card has a website, and the website has a mailing list.

What I thought was just an offline experience has now become online, and he's allowed me to become a loyal repeat customer.

UPDATED Customer Attributes -

Customer status: Current customer

Name: Mark

Age: 30–40

Interests: Craft beer, Hop plants.

NEW - Products: Hop plant.

NEW - Payment: Cash - Card preference

NEW - CLV: $10

NEW- Location: Local

NEW Audience List:

Local beer and hop lover.

New customer.

In this interaction, I genuinely enjoyed the experience. I was happy to exchange my information for a better customer experience and the passionate and insightful knowledge I received in the transaction. I was not the typical target market (at least, I didn't think so). Still, I have become a converted customer with a client lifetime value that I'm sure will steadily trickle up until I'm told I can't buy any more hop plants (because they take up too much room).

Different attributes are built over the customer's journey and lifetime to tailor personalised offers and content to specific audiences and to ensure the right message – at the right time or at least the best possible guess.

It's hoped that one day, brands will be able to emulate this natural, free flow of communication completely; that's what could be coming as part of Facebook's Metaverse instead of banana-mad billboard holders chasing you around. AI companies right now are working on bots intelligent enough to make you think they are your friend and then slowly introduce product mentions and encourage you to buy them. Skynet will not enslave the human race; it will convince us to purchase convertibles instead.

For now, we should set out with these types of valuable interactions and customer journeys in mind – working, where possible, to blur the lines between offline and online across our customer touchpoints and overall customer journey.

A Jack-Of-All-Trades And Master Of None

Apart from my stint in the markets, I got into marketing and advertising after university, studying Business and specialising in Marketing. It seemed like a path I was destined to go down, and of course, like most potential marketers, I was excited by big branding campaigns and stories featured on Madmen – the promise of big pitches, parties, and media lunches. By the time I got into marketing, the party seemed to have moved on or was moving on, or perhaps I just wasn't invited. A new type of marketer was crawling out from under the tables. Digital gave rise to social media, performance, and the completely mysterious search engine optimisers (SEOs) with their black and white hats. The point is that as media and marketing channels began expanding, so did the number of potential specialisations and potential hats a marketer could be expected to wear.

In digital, our challenge is compounded by the number of tools forever expanding into the market. At least with web analytics, things have been more or less contained with Google Analytics. Still, a marketing manager could be expected to know web analytics, user experience, update the website using a CMS, optimise tags for search engines, create and manage ads on Facebook and AdWords, and keep the socials moving on Instagram and Twitter. At the same time, they should set experiments in optimising tools while creating dashboards in Data Studio and all the traditional marketing functions and activities. The list of what you could or should be doing is endless, and I genuinely sympathise with business owners and marketing managers.

There is an endless stream of things that need to be done. Gone are the days of media lunches – we have work to do, and our bosses and clients expect solid, provable ROI, sales, and conversions. Of course, all this change and growth has brought tremendous opportunities, even if we struggle to keep up and often feel like a jack-of-all-trades and master of none.

As we progress through the Analytics Maturity Curve, we can feel like we don't have time to write measurement plans and maintain our analytics. It can mean we don't have the knowledge, skills, and abilities (KSAs) to do the job. As we progress through, the types of KSAs required continue to expand, and often, so does the team. We'll cover precisely who and what KSAs might be needed in Chapter 10 – Who is Missing.

3.2 – LET'S (FIRST-PARTY) DATA.

During and post-pandemic, our lives have been disrupted like never before, and the downstream effect of that has caused significant years for digital marketing. An initial Bank of America and Forrester study revealed that e-commerce jumped up to a 33% market share from 16% in 2019. Even now, if you are a brand or retailer, you are still probably suffering from the whiplash this caused on your marketing plans, your retail stores, and even your websites. We were reeling from 10 years of predicted growth in 3 months when that study came out. Had marketers seen this coming, how much would they have invested in their digital presence and infrastructure? During this time, customers have wanted more and more personalisation while simultaneously demanding more and more privacy online.

First-party data is information collected directly from a company's own customers or users, while third-party data is information collected by other companies. It matters now because privacy concerns and changes to data regulations have made first-party data more valuable and important for businesses as third-party data is increasingly less accessible.

Third-party tracking across devices and domains is being phased out to fit in with new government-led guidelines. More than ever, brands will need to develop better second-party and first-party data strategies and automation to serve their customers. They must meet higher expectations with less accessible data or risk losing out to competitors.

The Paradox

Personalisation VS Privacy and The Fragmenting Customer Journey

→ Customers expect greater personalisation. That could be more relevant and timely communication or a tailored onsite experience with personalized recommendations.

→ Customers expect brands to know them and provide personalised services and recommendations while simultaneously respecting their privacy.

→ Privacy concerns have led to the Fragmented Customer Journey through GDPR and increasing tracking difficulties - mainly 3rd party tracking.

Source McKtui Consulting

At first look, it does seem like a paradox. How can customers simultaneously be looking for greater personalisation but for companies to also not keep, store, or use any personal data about them?

That's oversimplifying the issue, and the truth is more nuanced. Some customers will want to be left alone entirely, some want to be messaged only on essential updates, and some customers aren't too bothered and are happy to be messaged on all things, including general offers. It comes down to their interest in the brand and the nature of the messages. There is also a trust and nurture element to this question: new customers may only want a little touch from your brand, but once they are converted, they may be happier to be more regularly exposed to your messages, especially if they have given permission and know that consent can be quickly rescinded.

This case study featuring Kmart, working with a Customer Data Platform provider, Telium, shows how to approach customers and lead with a best-practice approach.

Challenge:

Amid evolving data privacy regulations and increasing consumer demand for personalisation, Kmart sought to grant customers complete control over their data with a centralised consent management solution that enables compliant, personalised experience activation across all channels.

Solution:

'Tealium uniquely enabled Kmart to develop an innovative centralised consent management solution that unifies a customer's real-time consent status under a single customer profile. Kmart's centralised consent management solution resolved the issue of data fragmentation to unleash unlimited possibilities in the real-time cross-channel customer experience (CX). With a Tealium-enabled centralised consent management solution, Kmart enlisted Deloitte Digital to provide specialist consulting that accelerated data-driven CX innovation and impact with purpose and precision – combining Tealium's solutions with Deloitte Digital's specialist consulting, an innovation powerhouse that accelerated the time to market of Kmart's bespoke centralised consent management model.

'Results:

'Privacy by design unlocked the power of trust to build Kmart's personalisation engine. As the world's most trusted CDP, Tealium made data readily accessible and actionable, speeding up operations, saving costs and supporting growth, and making it easier to navigate compliance requirements. The result was an astounding 200% increase in Kmart's consenting customer base, substantially enhancing audience quality for improved relevance and conversions.

'Consent management is essential to the organisation of the future. With Tealium, Kmart has consolidated company-wide consent streams to deliver privacy-first customer experiences at every touchpoint. This approach has future-proofed our business to *remain compliant in an evolving regulatory landscape.'*

Photi Orfanidis – Architect, Marketing & Loyalty Technologies, Kmart Group Australia

'We live in a world where MarTech capabilities have rapidly grown to enable unlimited possibilities in personalisation. Yet, the only person truly qualified to validate our personalisation efforts is the customer.'

Dr Frederik De Keukelaere – Principal, Deloitte Digital

A first-to-market solution that puts consent at the heart of the customer experience

The volume of data at marketers' disposal is growing exponentially, and consumers have come to expect a fully personalised experience that recognises them as individuals. In the 'Internet of Everything' era, consumers make no distinction between their online and offline lives and do not expect companies to either. In parallel, evolving data privacy regulations, including the Consumer Data Right (CDR), necessitate a privacy-first approach to customer experience.

Kmart used Tealium as the foundation to build a first-to-market centralised consent management solution, positioning itself to adapt to future market challenges and gain a competitive edge. Kmart leveraged Tealium CDP to unify customers' consent status across all touchpoints, incorporating over 90 business and technical rules and 33 user flows. Consent has become an internal service, democratising data across the organisation and all third-party technologies via a centralised Consent Centre. While the back-end system is complex, the resulting product is simple and easy for staff, vendors, and consumers alike.

Tealium's Customer Data Hub and IQ Tag Management system enabled an intuitive and responsive customer experience. The solution was built on two components: unauthenticated cookie consent data and authenticated consent data. This increased transparency by allowing Kmart website visitors to manage their cookie data and Kmart account holders to choose whether personally identifiable information is used in a trusted value exchange. Kmart adopted a proprietary four-state logic system to resolve consent, whereby an express 'yes' or 'no' overwrites inferred or soft values. The system gives customers complete control over how their data is used and the level of real-time personalisation they receive across the retailer's channels.

Facing the future with transparency and agility

Putting privacy principles first has empowered Kmart to provide its customers with the desired experiences. With Tealium as the foundation of its technology stack, the retailer is future-ready and agile. Centralising customer consent from multiple sources has helped Kmart to establish a unified view of its first-, second-, and third-party data streams from multichannel activations. Kmart is now more transparent with its customers regarding how it tracks their data while restoring full control of that data to customers. As compliance and customer requirements become more complex, Kmart's future-ready centralised consent management solution extends beyond simply checking a box: it is what will drive competitive advantage in the privacy-first global data economy.

What I particularly like about this case study is, they start at the beginning. The first personalisation strategy any marketer should attempt is how to ensure customers can easily signal how, when, and what they want to be stored and used and ultimately, as Frederik De Keukelaere writes, 'the only person truly qualified to validate our personalisation efforts is the customer.'

Navigating the new world of digital marketing can be a daunting task, especially when it comes to explaining the value of services and making them relatable to all. A key challenge in selling SEO, for instance, is conveying its value and significance when executed correctly. The solution to this is to move beyond fancy titles and technical jargon and ground digital marketing in the real world. One effective way to achieve this is through the use of familiar examples and frameworks.

Contemporary digital marketing emphasises the importance of creating a human conversation on a larger scale. The goal is to replicate the natural customer experience of one human conversing with another individual, with the objective of building connections that ultimately result in sales. To achieve this, we must prioritise collecting first-party data.

While digital marketing has evolved tremendously over the years, the range of responsibilities that marketers must undertake continues to expand. As we advance through the Analytics Maturity Curve, the skills required to succeed in digital marketing continue to grow.

Despite the challenges, there are ample opportunities for those who are willing to adapt. One effective strategy to make digital marketing more accessible is to keep things simple by utilising familiar examples and frameworks and specialising where possible. It is crucial to remain open to learning and adapting as the industry continues to change, but it's clear that true growth lies in unlocking permission-based one-on-one conversations at scale – The Power of One.

◆ ◆ ◆

You should now have a more comprehensive understanding of some of the challenges we overworked and overburdened digital marketers experience, but also the tantalising opportunities available to any marketer or company that can effectively and ethically balance privacy and personalisation with the right value exchange and systems in place.

Next, as the **Cookie Apocalypse** looms, reshaping digital advertising, marketers must adapt to the demise of third-party cookies, embracing privacy-conscious strategies for personalised experiences. Brace for the future as we confront the cookie apocalypse head-on.

References And Bibliography

1. Tealium. (n.d.). Kmart and Tealium Put Consent First to Tackle the Personalisation Privacy Paradox [Case Study]. https://tealium.com/resource/case-study/kmart-and-tealium-put-consent-first-to-tackle-the-personalisation-privacy-paradox/

CHAPTER 4 – SURVIVING THE COOKIE APOCALYPSE

Now we're armed with some of these ideas, approaches, and frameworks, in this chapter, we'll get into the weeds with first-, second-, and third-party data, how it's linked to the coming Cookie Apocalypse, and why the foundations of digital marketing are about to be pulled away from underneath us.

I'll hit you with technical information but also support you with the must-have knowledge, what to consider, and why these decisions should not be left to your web developer or technical team.

4.1 – COOKIE MONSTER FOREVER

Unless you have been hiding your head in the sand, you know that third-party data is disappearing, someday, somehow and potentially that 'Cookies' and browser blocking have something to do with it. You may even have heard that server-side is the solution to all our problems.

There are times when you may need to loosely understand the absolute foundations of how all this works, how it's changing, and why. It can help us reason through potential issues, why your data will always, always be just a little bit F**ked, and why that's OK. We'll look at the causes, as well as how you should collect data in the future and questions you may need to ask. If you absorb anything, know that data collection is very flawed. **Your data should only be 90–95% accurate from any other comparable source, and that's OK.**

Third-party cookies and web browsers power pixel tracking, also called client-side tracking or cookie-based tracking. Cookies are simple, and web browsers do all the work of storing and sending information in pixel tracking, so it's easy to implement and use. Unfortunately, cookies are also easy for browsers to block, users to delete, and bad actors to leverage, leaving marketers and their campaigns at risk – not to mention that pixel tracking only works on desktop web, not mobile.

So, is the party over? For over 20 years third-party cookies have formed the bedrock of digital advertising, passed back and forth by publishers and advertisers, collected and stored unsuspectingly on all of our personal browsers. Our personal information and user behaviour could be used to target us without our permission or knowledge. Dialling up the internet signalled our acceptance, and if we wanted access to all this free information, there was a form of unwitting acknowledgement, like above-the-line media, that we would see some ads. Then it started getting creepy to the point that we are getting paranoid, but perhaps with good reason. Who has discussed a need for a product with a friend only to see an ad for it appear later on Facebook?

The move away from third-party cookies is gathering momentum as tech companies respond to growing consumer and regulatory concerns around personal data. Apple ended support for third-party cookies in Safari in 2018, and Google plans to do so in its Chrome browser by the end of 2023. This represents a tipping point since the two browsers between them have an 80% market share. Companies are being sued for using personal data without consent and, more recently, just for storing any customer data in countries outside of where the data was collected. Shit is getting real.

What are cookies, how much should I know, and why do I care? Search 'cookies', and you get something like this.

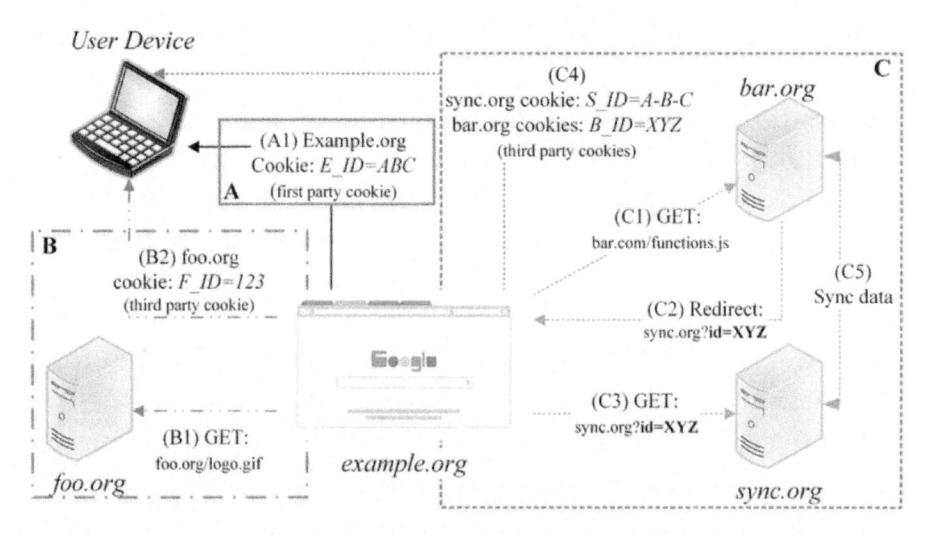

Source: The Unwanted Sharing Economy: An Analysis of Cookie Syncing and User Transparency under GDPR.

Different types of cookies: (A) a first-party cookie directly set by the visited website, (B) a third-party cookie set by a third party embedded in the website, and (C) a synchronised cookie shared between two parties.

Simple right? This is a problem for marketers. Although this is an excellent diagram for the experts, the concept of first-, second-, and third-party cookies is pretty esoteric, and even when you do get it, it changes because this is all still being worked out.

Remember, all this is considered client-side tracking. Let's start with the difference between each, why it's used, and examples of what comes under each category. Remember, whether something is first party or third party is in reference to the user on the website, and there are ongoing debates around what cookies should be considered first, second, or third party, including whether there are such things as second-party cookies. Many of these debates are being thrown around in the courtrooms right now, but it's safe to say companies don't want to be identified as 3rd parties if they can avoid it. We'll cover some of this in Section 8.3, Let's Go Tool Shopping – Data Sovereignty.

A user visits a website called news.com. Cookies placed on this domain by news.com are first-party cookies. A cookie placed by any other site, such as an advertiser or social media site, is a third-party cookie.

Web cookies: Different flavors

	FIRST-PARTY COOKIES	THIRD-PARTY COOKIES
WHO HOSTS	The domain you're visiting	Ad servers, social media sites, commenting aggregators, live-chat pop-ups, etc.
WHERE TRACKED	The domain you're visiting and, in rare instances, other sites	Users across many domains
MAIN PURPOSE	Smoother site access	Enabling adware
WHAT THEY DO	Remember logins, preferences, shopping cart items, etc.	Retarget prospective customers as they move from site to site

Source: TechTarget. (n.d.). What is a third-party cookie?

What Are First-Party Cookies?

When you visit a website, it may store information about your visit using cookies. These cookies are created and stored by the website you are visiting and are known as first-party cookies. They can store information about your session, viewed pages, items in your shopping cart, login credentials, or other preferences. The website developer decides what data points to collect to enhance your experience on their site. First-party cookies are stored under the same domain you are visiting, except in rare cases when other sites are involved.

What Are Third-Party Cookies?

Third-party cookies, on the other hand, are created and stored by websites that are not the ones you are currently visiting. They collect information about your online behaviour and browsing history and are often used by providers of advertising, retargeting, analytics, and tracking services. For example, if you were browsing shoes on shoe-in.com, a third-party cookie might store information about the products you viewed or added to your cart. This information could then be passed on to an ad server like DoubleClick. Later, when you visit another website like randomnewspaper.com, DoubleClick might use that information to display ads for shoes that you recently viewed. This is known as retargeting or remarketing.

Third-party cookies are set by servers, not by the websites that you are currently visiting.

When you visit a website such as shoe-in.com, it may load a piece of code from an ad server like DoubleClick that collects data about your visit to that site. If you then visit another site like randomnewspaper.com, that site may also load code from DoubleClick, which can identify you as the user who viewed shoes on shoe-in.com. Depending on shoe-in.com's advertising objectives, DoubleClick might then display an ad for shoes while you are browsing randomnewspaper.com. The newspaper website earns revenue from showing you ads based on the number of impressions, clicks, or purchases.

Technically there are only two types of cookies. Still, the cookie we used only partially fits into either category and, depending on the judge, often an actual judge, can be treated differently, thus resulting in data loss and screwy data. Our 'Web Cookies' example table says confidently that first-party cookies are 'tracked' on or by the domain you're on – e.g. randomshop.com. However, Google Analytics uses www.google-analytics.com/collect to send data to other servers, often across state and country lines, and we regularly use GA for cross-domain tracking. The difference is that in most browsers, these cookies are set as being on the 'allow list', even if they don't match the URL of the host domain (the website that is first-party to the user). This potential mismatch is happening on the client side.

Second-Party Cookies

This is where an argument is presented that an agreement can be made to share data from one to another from the first party to the second. As long as the original website user has given permission, this can be considered second-party, almost extending the rights of a first party to what would otherwise be regarded as a third party. We're saying, 'hey, they're with us. I know them'.

What Are Second-Party Cookies?

Second-party cookies are not really considered cookies. There are either first- or third-party cookies – cookies that are either stored by the domain you're visiting or by another domain (like the shoe-in.com example). It means two parties who agreed to share cookies. So, you have a first-party cookie stored by the website you visited. The whole file is then transferred to another party by mutual agreement or partnership. As discussed, this is all considered 'client-side' tracking.

Server-Side Tracking

Unlike Pixel and JavaScript SDK tracking, server-side tracking or postback tracking does not rely on web browsers to work. Postback tracking uses direct server communication instead, also called server-side tracking or server-to-server tracking. This frees marketers from cookie-based browser restrictions and provides complete control over campaign tracking. It also works better cross-channel on the desktop web, mobile web, and mobile apps.

Server-side tracking dates back to the early 1990s when website statistics consisted primarily of counting the number of client requests (or hits) made to the web server. Web servers record some of their transactions in a log file. It was soon realised that these log files could be read by a program to provide data on the website's popularity.

To get around this problem of client-side cookies and to enable safer and more accurate data collection, Google and other companies began introducing more readily accessible server-side technologies, and this is where the lines continued to blur. On June 30, 2020, Google released the server-side Google Tag Manager. Server-side tagging allows Tag Manager users to move measurement tag instrumentation out of their website or app and into server-side processing via Google Cloud.

It seems Google was set for server-side tracking, but very few companies have made the transition as yet. Google has just declared their cookies first-party. Even with the coming tracking solutions server-side, if the data appears in Google servers as well as our own (with permission from our customers), then Google is still a third party; perhaps second based on agreement and permission, but is not first party, and it really should always come down to consent.

Server-side tracking solves the tracking issue by getting past the coming browser restrictions and third-party tracking limitations by moving data collection behind a veil. However, it does not answer the ethical, data sovereignty, and permission-based questions; these still need to be addressed.

Focus on the core permission issue first, and you won't go far wrong. See this as just a technical issue to be hacked, and you may open yourself to legal consequences or have all your hard work become too risky and be thrown out. There are some large organisations on this type of rope, but for obvious reasons, I shall not name them.

Fingerprinting And Blackhat Seo

I can't think of a more cynical approach than Fingerprinting in analytics other than yesterday's one-trick ponies, SEO black-hatters. Short-term strategies like this couldn't be missing the point by any more. They are more about cutting corners and quick gains than solving a problem or offering lasting value. They are, at worst, a con and, at best, a stalling technique.

Search engine optimisation (SEO) has forever been a slow march from black-hat manipulation of search algorithms to supporting search engines in delivering the best content for customers. An algorithm decides what content ranks first and what content does not; those experts in SEO worked hard to understand and game the algorithm creating spammy fake links and terrible content only designed to fool the algorithm and, for a short time, make lots of money doing it.

Unfortunately for their clients, these tricks became less and less effective as the algorithm got better and better. Soon, the whole industry became cost ineffective, and all that work became useless, often all at once in dramatic business-destroying algorithm updates like Google Panda and Penguin.

The algorithm got better and better at ranking hard-earned quality content. At what point should companies have worked to provide better content rather than paying more specialists for short-term gains or to recover past losses? There are learnings here on how to approach the modern tracking issues, and it boils down to this: don't work against the trend; instead, anticipate it.

While it is possible to block third-party cookies using your browser, server-side browser fingerprinting, also known as digital or online fingerprinting, cannot be blocked in the same way. By analysing your device and settings, a fingerprinting algorithm can determine your identity or make an educated guess about it and create a profile based on your online behaviour. Even though it may not be able to identify you by name or face, like cookies, it can still monitor your activity across various browsing sessions and track you across the internet.

Browser fingerprinting is capable of gathering a vast amount of information about your device, including the browser you are using, your time zone, operating system, screen resolution, device hardware, and more. The multitude of data points collected is what makes fingerprinting so effective and potentially problematic.

Unlike third-party cookies, browser fingerprinting isn't regulated, so websites have no legal incentive to abstain from using it. And since it uses scripts that look just like the ones websites need to function, it's tough to detect. Google and other companies are moving towards blocking it, but they are only some of the way there.

4.2 – SOLUTIONS AND POSSIBLE DATA STRATEGIES

What does this all mean to us marketers, and how should we use this information to make decisions about our data? If we want our data to be less F**ked up than it is now and to ensure we're future-proofed for as long as possible, we must have the right data strategy in place.

Most agree it's time to steadily move to server-side tracking, but we need to do this with permission at the heart of the decision. It's no longer enough to say we're collecting the data for website improvements, as we'll see later. We also need to review when choosing our tools where that data is stored and who other than ourselves has access to the data – again offering our customers the opportunity of opting in and out. But we also need to have an agreed data strategy to guide our decision-making and inform everyone in the company of where we stand across each type of data and strategy.

Possible Data Strategies

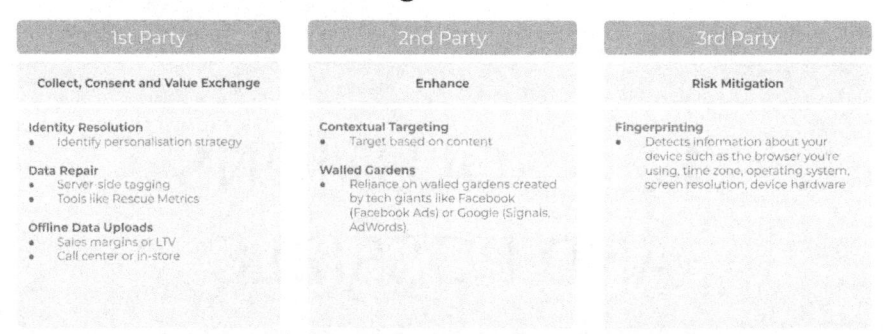

1st Party	2nd Party	3rd Party
Collect, Consent and Value Exchange	Enhance	Risk Mitigation
Identity Resolution • Identify personalisation strategy **Data Repair** • Server-side tagging • Tools like Rescue Metrics **Offline Data Uploads** • Sales margins or LTV • Call center or in-store	**Contextual Targeting** • Target based on content **Walled Gardens** • Reliance on walled gardens created by tech giants like Facebook (Facebook Ads) or Google (Signals, AdWords)	**Fingerprinting** • Detects information about your device such as the browser you're using, time zone, operating system, screen resolution, device hardware

Source: McKTui Consulting – Based on Marketing in a world without third-party cookies. Colleen Rose.

There will be several tactics we should employ and some we should just be aware of and avoid. The core of any longer-term strategy must be to collect first-party data; we do this by offering something of value in exchange for using that data. Bit by bit, we'll build up a clearer resolution of who our customers are, but only to better serve them as only as far as they are comfortable.

Where we're still using client-side collection, we can steadily test and increase the use of server-side tracking or even use additional tools that work to supplement and repair client-side tracking, such as Rescue Metrics. However, again, we should have permission to do this, and, like our examples, we will look to bring on additional sources of data, such as offline data uploads.

Where required and however defined, we will need to balance our strategy with second-party strategies: working in partnership (albeit very one-sided) with the big tech giants, their first-party data, and their walled gardens. This could be where we have a list of customers collected through first-party tracking and then upload the list, with permission, to Facebook to continue the conversation.

Finally, let's all agree, here and now, not to be creepy – if only because it could cost your company much more money when the hacks stop working or you eventually end up in court. We won't pursue third-party strategies or use server-side tracking for the wrong reasons. We'll adopt a risk mitigation policy and ensure it's part of an actual data policy.

All this should be tied into the business and marketing strategy, our positioning, and our promise to our customers (Chapter 7 – Picking a Strategy). As an organisation, let's decide not to circumvent cookies and first-party tracking with server-side tracking or fingerprinting because we can or because it's an easier fix. But instead, let's do better as part of our mission to serve our customers and clients better. We need to have the conversation at least and understand a little, if not everything, of some of this boring data collection stuff. The method is just as important as the mission. Please take me back to the days of media lunches.

◆ ◆ ◆

With a broader understanding of the technological and political pressures driving the fragmented customer journey, we now explore the essential data strategies for moving forward.

Tracking and collecting data become crucial, emphasising the significance of both our methods and mission.

Next, we outline the **Pillars of Personalisation**, treating data as a resource, applying analytics maturity, and navigating available tools. Prepare to redefine your approach and embrace a transformative journey towards effective personalisation.

References And Bibliography

1. PerformanceIN. (2020). First-party vs. third-party tracking cookies: What they are and why you should drop them. https://performancein.com/news/2020/09/15/first-party-vs-third-party-tracking-cookies-what-they-are-and-why-you-should-

drop-them/#:~:text=Pros%3A%20Easy%20to%20set%20up,%2C%20and%20soon%20Google's%20Chrome).
2. CHOICE. (n.d.). Browser fingerprinting and the death of third-party cookies. https://www.choice.com.au/consumers-and-data/data-collection-and-use/who-has-your-data/articles/browser-fingerprinting-and-death-of-third-party-cookies
3. Basgösewisch, A. (2021). First, second and third-party cookies: What it all means. https://basgosewisch.com/first-second-and-third-party-cookies-what-it-all-means/
4. TechTarget. (n.d.). What is third-party cookie? - Definition from WhatIs.com. https://www.techtarget.com/whatis/definition/third-party-cookie
5. Information Commissioner's Office. (2021). What are cookies and similar technologies? Guidance on the use of cookies and similar technologies. https://ico.org.uk/for-organisations/guide-to-pecr/guidance-on-the-use-of-cookies-and-similar-technologies/what-are-cookies-and-similar-technologies

CHAPTER 5 – THE PILLARS OF PERSONALISATION

Discover how the Pillars of Personalisation propel us along the Analytics Maturity Curve. Through a Risk and Readiness Review, we assess Analytics Maturity, Data as a Resource, and Tools and Technology.

Explore their relationship to our Ferrari analogy, ensuring a memorable and comprehensive understanding of this framework. Unleash the power of personalisation and fuel your path to Analytics Maturity.

5.1 – THE PARTHENON TO SUSTAINABLE GROWTH

There are three critical pillars required for effective and sustainable personalisation, and our data and personalisation strategies rest upon these foundational pillars. Each is equally important, although additional capability in one area can compensate for lack of capability in another. Like the Parthenon, without all the pillars in place, the structure, in this case your marketing growth and personalisation strategies, will be unstable. If we lack in an area, we'll find it impossible to get any personalisation project off the ground at all.

Pillars to Personalisation

```
                    Growth

            Personalisation Strategy

      ┌────────┐  ┌─────────┐  ┌──────────┐
      │  Data  │  │Available│  │ Analytics│
      │Resource│  │  Tools  │  │ Maturity │
      └────────┘  └─────────┘  └──────────┘

              Marketing Strategy
              Business Strategy
```

Source: McKtui Consulting

To explain this memorably, let's crowbar in another metaphor here. Think of a car; the car is a brand-new Ferrari. It's a Ferrari because everyone knows a Ferrari is fast, powerful, and effective at what it is designed to do. Hopefully, your strategies do not cost the same as a Ferrari.

OK, so you have a Ferrari. It's fantastic, with all the bells and whistles. It goes 218 miles per hour and has leather seats and an infrared cigarette lighter. For our sake, this could be a fully-implemented CDP, CRM system, Webtools, real-time recording of users' sessions, directly accessible by a call centre, advanced self-service dashboards connected to all our customer and business data – and there is lots of data, fantastic data all expertly linked by a federated ID, with very little data loss and full permissions. You're revving, raring and ready to go.

What do you do? How do you do it? Where do you go? Do you try four things simultaneously in an attempt to appease everyone else sitting in the car? Do you try to pursue the recommendations from the CEO's daughter or be influenced by just the highest-paid person's opinion (HIPPO)? Analytics maturity, as we've reviewed, covers many different areas, but most of them are centred around having the right people and process with the knowledge, skills, and abilities (KSA) to ensure that we take the optimal path and make solid, informed strategic decisions; otherwise, we are going to waste a lot of time and money; not only that, we could do more damage than good to the brand.

Pillars to Personalisation

Source: McKTui Consulting

Tools And Drivers – No Fuel

OK, here is an alternative: you have all the tools, the Ferrari is still ready to go, and now you know what to do with it; Mario Andretti (arguably the best racing car driver of all time) is sitting behind the wheel with a full pit crew, and everyone is aligned – now that's exciting and the sky's the limit. But then you realise you've got no fuel; pretty impressive how you missed it, but the tank is full of a mixture of tar and gravy, and all the data coming in is junk. Some could be refined, but it is useless and flawed for your purposes.

Most likely, if you had the team worked up to higher levels of analytics maturity, you would not have made it to this stage of development. Still, it could be that you have lost your key data sources to recent legal or social changes, or perhaps you paid other organisations for their time in implementing your stack and their time as an extension of your team and didn't stop to ask what you are going to do with this technology and what data you need to be collecting to get there.

You've got a fancy Ferrari, an expert team, and a driver without the data it needs to run. This could be particularly true if your company invested heavily in programmatic and DMPs, which traditionally required vast amounts of freely available third-party data to be effective.

Drivers And Fuel – No Tools

Finally, and this is the most exciting prospect for any SaaS salesperson, you have loads of great data and the in-house experience to understand what their product does and how to use it. You've got a pit team of Ferrari enthusiasts ready to go and some rich, exciting data ready to be used and integrated, with customers waiting to hear from you and willing for you to use their data.

In reality, it will never be entirely just one of these situations. Still, the model gives an easy way for us to explain and understand the different areas required to move forward, what could happen, and why we need to improve in one of the pillars somehow.

A good start for any organisation is to pull the various siloed stakeholders together and work through a Risk and Readiness Review. This could be a series of meetings or, ideally, a facilitated workshop to get the most out of your team. By evaluating your cross-functional teams, you can gauge where you are in each pillar and where to invest resources first. Follow-up sessions can be conducted after any initial investment in tools, data, or people to assess progress or as part of an annual or monthly cycle. By taking an initial benchmark before you start and having structured reviews, you can reassess and track your progress together and discuss any trouble areas or unexpected issues.

Risk And Readiness Review – Exercise

The Risk and Readiness Review

Risk and Readiness Review – Led by a web analytics specialist, this aims to quantify the organisation's readiness and risks. We look at possible opportunities and threats across four key areas: Data as a Resource, Tools and the MarTech Stack, Analytics Maturity, and Risk. It should take 45 minutes with time for open discussion.

Shoe-in.com and team.

Here is an example of a Risk and Readiness Review. In this chapter, you will learn how to recreate your own review in a spreadsheet and work through it as a team, adding up the scores for each section as you go and then finalising those scores at the end. Each group member can add their score to be included in the whole. Over time, by adding a multiplier, I have modified this sheet to increase or decrease the importance of some questions, but it's sufficient to create and benchmark a line in the sand from which to work.

We're ultimately looking to achieve a rough score of our readiness with a breakdown for each pillar to identify some initial key opportunities for us to explore further and an initial assessment of the potential risks of not addressing the possible issues and moving forward.

Your Score Card - Readiness and Opportunity

Risk and Readiness Review – Led by a Web Analytics Specialist, this aims to quantify the organizations readiness and risks we look at possible opportunities and threats across four key areas: Data as Resource, Tools and the MarTech Stack, Analytics Maturity and Risk.

Key Opportunities

→ Readiness at 60% - Good with room for improvement.
  - Opportunity for improved integration using Available Tools such as HubSpot.
  - Data Resources likely undervalued lower score due to lacking unique IDs and Logged in/Logged out data. Value Exchange very promising.
  - Support needed in Governance, Objectives, Scope and Improvement process methodology - current team stretched.
  - Target to get from level 3 to level 4 in 12 months. This requires better integration of existing tools.

Score Card

Readiness	60%
Analytics Maturity	52%
Available Tools	79%
Data Resource	50%

Source: McKTui Consulting

5.2 – ANALYTICS MATURITY AS AN ORGANISATION

A great place to start is your organisation's analytics maturity, directly linked to the Analytics Maturity Curve in the previous chapter – not only where our organisation is on the curve but what kinds of roles and responsibilities may be required at this stage. Before starting, ask yourself:

1. Where do we sit on the Analytics Maturity Curve now?
2. Where do we want to be in 6–12 months? Or two years? Or five years?

Once you have your team together, here are some initial statements to rate your organisation. It relates to the freely available Cardinal Path self-analysis, which I strongly recommend reviewing.

Risk and Readiness Review

Data Resource - Opportunity	1	2	3	4	5	Average
Web Data - Answer considering whether the data is accessible and trustworthy						
Session/Pageviews		2	3	4	5	1	3.0
Bounce Rate/Time on Page						
Events/Conversions						

Source: McKtui Consulting

We Trust Our Data

A great question to quickly align or divide the room is scoring how much we trust our data. For some people, this may be the first time they learn that there is a problem and the data is F**ked. They've been using it for months.

Governance

We have well-defined, well-communicated roles and responsibilities, holding teams and people accountable across the full spectrum of activities required to collect, analyse, and use data to measure and act on business goals.

By asking this, not only do we want to know if this is in place, but do others know it's in place? Quite commonly, a manager might say yes, this is all done but be frustrated to learn that nobody knows where it is or references it. This is why scoring individually, discussing, and noting where there is misalignment is essential.

Objectives

We have very clear business objectives that are measured by structured Key Performance Indicators (KPIs) designed to quantify success or failure.

Targets might also exist in some areas and not in others, or sometimes, when bringing two teams together, it is suddenly apparent that their objectives conflict.

Scope

We have spread analysis activities throughout their entire digital ecosystem and are actively leveraging analytics as an organisation-wide programme for transformational change.

The critical success factor here concerns the whole organisational change and whether the implementation is siloed. Often marketing can be at odds with IT, especially if IT is more concerned with more business administrative tasks or implementations such as POS, ERP, or company-wide 'data lake' projects. IT might see marketing as just another data point or team.

Team

We include the technical implementation resources, experienced analysts, and data architects; in addition, the business users are empowered and experienced in data-driven decision-making methodologies.

It is excellent to get an initial feeling. Do we have the people we need to achieve our goals, and who might be missing for projects in the future?

Improvement Process Methodology

We include formal frameworks such as Agile (Lean) or Six Sigma across our teams and departments and enable team members to learn and use these frameworks to ensure continuous improvements are being made throughout the organisation.

It will be straightforward if Agile or Six Sigma is part of your process. If you don't know what this is, don't worry; we're casting the net wide here to see the possible improvement areas.

Tools And Technology And Data Integration

We use tools and technology to enable data-derived insights from intelligent reporting, useful visualisations, statistical modelling, and even predictive analytics (mark your answer out of five).

This is an excellent initial question to get us to think about this before we cover Tools and Tech and start reviewing our MarTech Stack.

Sometimes you don't know what you don't know, and this process is a great way to identify possible gaps.

Ultimately our organisation's analytics maturity will depend on the strategic leadership and how clearly our goals are communicated, picking a strategy (Chapter 7), good planning (Chapter 6) and our team (Chapter 10).

5.3 – DATA AS A RESOURCE

As business models evolve, more companies will probably find that data is their biggest asset. The questions below help us understand and grow this asset.

1. What are your greatest existing or potential data resources?
2. Is that offline or online?
3. What benefits would a potential or existing customer have from sharing their data with you?

British mathematician Clive Humby famously said in 2006, 'Data is the new oil.'

Clive Humby is a British mathematician who established Tesco's Clubcard loyalty programme. Humby highlighted that, although inherently valuable, data needs processing, just as oil needs refining before its actual value can be unlocked.

Although another great visual, data is arguably more renewable, there is an abundance of it in most places, and the challenges are more to do with collecting, storing, and making it useful. The important point is that data should be seen as valuable – as valuable as the profit and revenue it can generate rather than just the maintenance and development costs on a balance sheet.

We looked at the recent Cannes winner Data Tienda. This is an excellent example of a data resource the organisation didn't know was possible. In this case, they had to collect the needed data, but the *eureka* moment was realising that they could uniquely collect the data and put it to great use.

So how can we review our data resource? A good start is to list common data sources for marketers and start discussing across our silos whether we have access to the data and feel it's trustworthy. A score of one could indicate totally F**ked, or perhaps we're not sure if we can or should use it, and five would indicate that it ticks all the four Data P's and is suitable for us to work into our plans.

Because we will need to get permission to use our customers' data, the important point is to include the value exchange in the discussion: what can we offer customers for this data now and in the future? Are they genuinely going to get a better-personalised experience, and if so, how will that work? Or might we offer a free version of our services, gated content, or some customer dashboard that regularly expects them to log in?

There are also data points in the list that will be more important than others; for example, Bounce Rate is steadily becoming unimportant, and the metric is no longer used in GA4 because it was often unreliable (or at least misunderstood). Any data points where we can collect identifying information become much more critical as they allow us to start tying all our touch points and channels together to one user or person, even if that person prefers to remain nothing more than a unique but random identifier such as a numeric code, rather than sharing their name or email.

Ultimately, we want to work towards a Federated ID. I'm not a massive Lord of the Rings fan, but enough people are for this example to work, and enough lore is known for at least a partial connection, be it with raised eyebrows or a bemused expression; but trust me, after reading this, the concept will stick.

> **" One Ring to rule them all,
> One Ring to find them,
> One Ring to bring them all."**
>
> —J.R.R. Tolkien's epigraph to The Lord of the Rings

Imagine each of these rings as unique identifiers; they may be email addresses from the app, a cookie ID from the website, or a code generated by your POS or back-end system, but ultimately, we need One to Rule Them All: one point of reference with a one-to-many connection. This should not be any kind of personally identifiable information as we will end up using it many times, in many systems and tools, and ultimately it can be used to trace back to PII if known (stored somewhere appropriately safe like a secure data warehouse or trusted CRM system); this is what we mean by a Federated ID.

A federated identity in information technology links a person's electronic identity and attributes stored across multiple identity management systems. It could be a separate standalone service like that offered by using your Google password or Facebook password (remember our discussion about walled gardens of data).

One example of federated identity is when users log into a third-party website using their Gmail login credentials. With FIM (FIM is a secure system for user authorisation, authentication, and digital identity management), they don't have to create new credentials to access multiple websites that have a federated agreement with Google, such as:

- YouTube
- Fitbit
- Waze
- Picasa
- Blogger

Similarly, a user can use their Facebook credentials to log into many websites that are federated with Facebook, like:

- Instagram
- Netflix
- Disney+

...or it could be used in your CPD or data warehouse to order and organise all your other unique identifiers.

Data is valuable but comes at a cost, so we need a strategy around how to use and maintain our data. It's also a resource that can be built and improved over time. We may sit down and create a measurement plan that intends to track everything so that we can use all that data with help from AI or by building all the more minor data points into an overall score. Still, if it doesn't have value now or immediately, the actual collection of that data should come later.

Finally, our data is only as valuable as our data practices because the better our practices, the less likely it is that our data will be F**ked.

It is not enough to have data. You need Data Governance – a commonly understood and consistently executed set of principles for managing data. Organisations should pay attention to the following four principles to create good data practices and avoid data-related fires, which can be included in our project plan. For now, let's also ask ourselves.

Data Provenance (where did my data come from?)

Data Privacy (what am I allowed to do with this data?)

Data Protection (how can I make sure I don't lose the data?)

Data Preparation (how do I go from data to valuable knowledge?)

Next is to look at our tools and tech – the Ferrari in our analogy.

5.4 – TOOLS AND TECH

Countless software tools are being created to serve this newly forming Marketing Stack, but which tools are good for what? Do I need a CRM, ETL, CDP, TMS, or DMP tool or a Data Warehouse on top of my web analytics tool? And does anyone know what those acronyms stand for?

1. What tool or tools is more important to your existing marketing efforts?

This could be AdWords, GA, HubSpot, Mailchimp, Big Query – anything you use as part of your MarTech structure.

2. What do you think is the tool you miss most in achieving your goals?

Available Tools - Opportunity

MarTech Stack – Your tech stack refers to the list of tools or platforms that your company uses to achieve different marketing, sales, and operational goals.

Customer Data Platform: eg Segment
Data Management Platform: Double Click
Advertising Tools: AdWords
Email Marketing Tools: Mailchimp
Social Media Platform: Facebook/Facebook/LinkedIn/Twitter
CRM: HubSpot/Salesforce
Marketing Automation Tools: HubSpot/Salesforce/Blaze/Marketo

Source: McKtui Consulting.

Using our Risk and Readiness framework, here are some key tool types to evaluate in your potential MarTech Stack.
- Customer Data Platform: e.g. Segment
- Data Management Platform: e.g. Double Click
- Advertising Tools: e.g. AdWords
- Email Marketing Tools: e.g. Mailchimp
- Social Media Platform: e.g. Facebook/LinkedIn/Twitter
- CRM System: e.g. HubSpot/Salesforce
- Marketing Automation Tools: e.g. HubSpot/Salesforce/Blaze/Marketo
- Web Analytics: e.g. Google Analytics/Matamo/Mixpanel/ Tealeaf/ Hotjar
- Tag Management System: e.g. GTM
- Self-Service Dashboards: e.g. Data Studio/ Tableau/ Power BI
- Data Warehouse: e.g. Redshift/Big Query/Snowflake

This is by no means an exhaustive list, but it captures some key tool types with examples of how and when they may act as other tools and serve their core function. See the glossary for a comprehensive description of each. I've deliberately kept any acronyms where the acronym is more often used than speaking or writing out the actual words. In Chapter 8 (Let's Go Tool Shopping), we'll go into much more detail about creating your own solution design and making good decisions on what tools should be included in your stack and when.

Let's start by looking at CDPs and how they differ from other tools and can help mitigate some of the possible risks of over-investing or locking into one particular vendor.

A CDP is part of the stack that specialises in connecting all the other tools, and that connective ability is the unique selling point and function of this tool. Segment is one of the most popular CDP providers, so it's uniquely positioned to research the most commonly used tool connections: those tools marketers like using. These will be tools that have good connections to this particular CDP, but the example is still illustrative.

'For the third year running, analytics tools dominate the most popular apps on the Segment platform. Mixpanel is an excellent alternative to GA; its primary use is giving greater data sovereignty and more detailed product-specific analytics:'

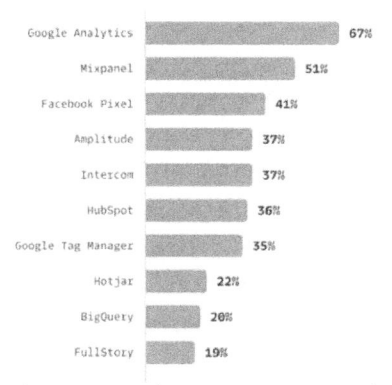

App	%
Google Analytics	67%
Mixpanel	51%
Facebook Pixel	41%
Amplitude	37%
Intercom	37%
HubSpot	36%
Google Tag Manager	35%
Hotjar	22%
BigQuery	20%
FullStory	19%

Source: Segment (n.d.). The CDP report. https://segment.com/the-cdp-report/

'Moving down the list, Google's BigQuery has entered the top ten for the first time. We anticipate this trend will continue as a growing percentage of customers deploy cloud warehouse solutions alongside a CDP to fully activate the power of their data.'

But what were the fastest growing apps in 2022 according to Segment?

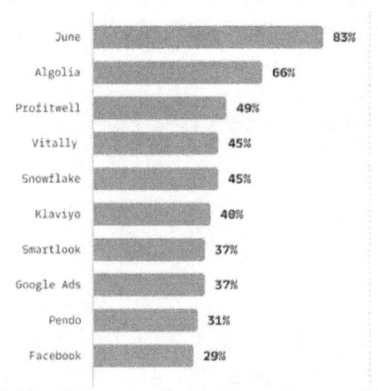

Tool	Percentage
June	83%
Algolia	66%
Profitwell	49%
Vitally	45%
Snowflake	45%
Klaviyo	40%
Smartlook	37%
Google Ads	37%
Pendo	31%
Facebook	29%

Source: Segment. (n.d.). The CDP report. https://segment.com/the-cdp-report/

June, for those interested, is an extensive business solution for creating newsletters and landing pages; combined with flexible marketing automation, it's attractive for marketers without any coding skills or support from developers. This may be great for marketing, but what about IT? Furthermore, what if only one person in the organisation knows how June works because it is so new?

To map out what tools we need in our MarTech Stack and outside, we need to draft a Solution Design and have the logic of the tools chosen interrogated by all levels of the organisation.

The balance we want to strike with a marketing stack has to be on trend with where things are going; everything around us is becoming more specialised and interconnected.

According to Brian Kardon, author of *CRM is Not Enough*, 'With the rise of the cloud, open source, the API economy, and digital everything, the landscape is becoming more fragmented, not less, and will continue to be so over the coming years. We think best-of-breed beats Jenga-tower-suites and are building our software and systems to work with, not against, each other.'

A CRM system may or may not be the solution, but it can never and should never be the only solution for your organisation. If it is, you have put too much trust in one provider or missed an important part of your stack.

Now we know how to structure our approach working up the Analytics Maturity Curve by using the Pillars to Personalisation working steadily towards the Power of One – sounds a bit like psychic mumbo jumbo – we can start writing and putting our plans into action. If you work for an agency, this could be part of a proposal, and if you are on the client side or an owner-operator, this might be a business case.

◆ ◆ ◆

We've come to grasp the complexities of the data landscape and acknowledge its current state. Now, it's time to transition from understanding to action.

Together, we'll embark on an approach that redefines our strategy, uncovering the exciting possibilities that arise from this new era of permission-led and cooperative working methods.

Next up, it is time to **Take Action** in Part Two of this book.

Reference And Bibliography

1. Rigby, D. K., Reichheld, F. F., & Schefter, P. (2002). Avoid the four perils of CRM. Harvard Business Review, 80(2), 101-109. https://hbr.org/2002/02/avoid-the-four-perils-of-crm
2. Kardon, B. (2018). CRM is not enough. Segment. https://segment.com/blog/crm-is-not-enough/
3. Talagala, N. (2022). Data as the new oil is not enough: Four principles for avoiding data fires. Forbes. https://www.forbes.com/sites/nishatalagala/2022/03/02/data-as-the-new-oil-is-not-enough-four-principles-for-avoiding-data-fires/?sh=3fc228e4c208
4. OneLogin. (n.d.). Federated identity: Definition, benefits, and how it works. https://

www.onelogin.com/learn/federated-identity
5. LoTR – One Ring Mythology Explained [Video]. (2018). YouTube. https://www.youtube.com/watch?v=WKU0qDpu3AM
6. Source: Segment. (n.d.). The CDP report. https://segment.com/the-cdp-report/
7. Booth, D. Analytics Maturity Model: A Framework for Success. Published on the Cardinal Path blog. Available at: https://www.cardinalpath.com/blog/a-model-for-mature-web-analytics

PART TWO – TAKING ACTION

Congratulations, you made it through to here. Let's make this count.

Part Two is all about taking action. We will build on the frameworks, examples, and foundations from Part One. Insufficient planning is one of the most common reasons for any project to go wrong, and our analytics are the same. What is staggering about this industry is how much money is spent on advertising without proper planning.

Working on many personalisation projects, I've made mistakes, but each mistake has led to a better result and process. This first chapter of Part Two, **Plan, Plan, Plan**, includes the summary of all that work. Every issue, problem, or 'I wish we'd thought of that' and 'we should do this differently next time'. **It all went into this framework, and now it's all yours.** Some of the content has been moved to the additional resources appendix for readability. Still, I wanted it there as I fully expect you to come back to this chapter time and time again when planning your project and learning each time from your mistakes. Everything you need is here for your successful digital transformation.

In **Picking a Strategy**, we'll look at personalisation and data strategies and how important it is to have clear business and marketing-level strategies. In this chapter, we'll assume that you have the power to inform and persuade business-level decisions and develop your own personalisation data and growth strategy but are ultimately dependent on a given business or marketing-level directives with associated KPIs. If you also control those too, fantastic; if not, we'll look at what you will need for possible 'up management' solutions – i.e. doing your boss's job for them. We'll examine why the price of light is less than the cost of darkness and the **serious risk** that you may be running without even knowing it.

We'll go **tool shopping**, take a cold hard look at SaaS sales pitches, and ask some serious questions about how best to organise our tools and MarTech Stack. Should we invest in off-the-shelf tools or look to create custom in-house solutions? **Do we need a CRM system,** and how much should we invest in one? What is Data Sovereignty, and why is it much less boring than it sounds? Together, we'll plan the likely real cost of these tools, strategies, and considerations for individual tools from someone who has used them and worked with hundreds of people who have also used them and shared their personal experiences.

In **Reporting vs. Dashboarding**, we'll push past the common and misleading distractions of dashboard design, use a structured strategic approach analysing who needs what data and when, and discuss if they should actually have it. As we move through the Analytics Maturity Curve, we'll seek to move through the DIKW Pyramid (I'm honestly not making all these up). How do we get from Data to Wisdom, and what does that mean?

Finally, we can't do this all ourselves. So what could an internal or external team look like? What are the **different roles and titles involved** in a typical project, and when do we bring on different knowledge, skills, and abilities effectively and affordably?

If this book was a rollercoaster, after a short bump, you are about to hit the drop; buckle up!

CHAPTER 6 – PLAN, PLAN, PLAN

In this chapter, we'll go behind the scenes and explore an example project and all the valuable documentation and plans needed to navigate a digital transformation project. The documentation can be broadened out or dialled back depending on the size and complexity of your solution and plans for the future.

We'll look at the essential **Project Plans, Solution Designs, and time-saving Code, Metrics, and Dimension Libraries.**

We'll look at the **Measurement Plan**, and you'll wonder why you don't have one of your own.

You can choose to ignore it, but after reading this, you can never feign ignorance again. Take what you need and use what you can.

6.1 – PLAN OR PLAN TO FAIL

One of the most common reasons for any project to go wrong is insufficient planning, and of course, our analytics are the same. What is staggering about this industry is how much money is spent on advertising without sufficient SMART (specific, measurable, attainable, realistic, trackable) planning, and even more, it's criminal how much is spent without good data or easy-to-understand reporting, targets, and KPIs. In this chapter, we'll look at the areas of planning required for steady movement up the Analytics Maturity Curve and ensuring our data is as unF**ked as possible.

The documentation can be broadened out or dialled back depending on the size and complexity of your solution and plans for the future. Still, there should be some mention in your planning – even if just one line – on each area addressed below, and some documents, like the Measurement Plan, should be seen as non-negotiable.

1. Project Plan
2. Communication Plan
3. Solution Design
4. Measurement Plan and Checklist
5. Custom Metric and Dimension Library
6. Code Library and Developer Instructions
7. Ongoing Governance and Testing
8. Reporting Structure and Strategy

6.2 – PROJECT PLAN – THE UNWRITTEN

The greater level of customisation from available toolsets often increases the requirement for additional documentation. The documentation is needed to ensure that the solution does not become too reliant on too few people.

The Project and Communication Plan outlines the overall strategy for the supporting tasks and project. The finished document aims to define clearly:

1. The overall strategy
2. The problem or opportunity
3. The scope of what we are looking to achieve
4. The timeline by asset
5. Responsibility and risks for the project
6. Communication Plan

This document should be freely shared with all your stakeholders to ensure you can communicate what you want to achieve and when.

In this example, we're going to work through a hypothetical situation. Shoe-in.com has big plans to integrate its data sources to offer effective personalisation. The big idea with Shoe-in is that you can design and edit various product lines of shoes online and have those shoes made to order. Shoes can be sent to you or further customised and fitted in-store. This is common for Shoe-in customers. They have offline retail stores – with a loyalty programme that regularly collects information about their customers through the point-of-sale (POS) system. They have grown fast, often run too fast, and take on too much at a time, never with adequate planning, governance, and documentation. This is their NEW project plan.

Strategic Priority

Through discussions with key stakeholders, we have agreed on shoe-in.com's highest priority needs. Work should support the following requirements for understanding and improving the online booking experience across assets, from the existing platforms to the offline in-store customer experience. The key business needs are:

1. Expand the width of tracking and GA3/GA4 – For internal understanding, Shoe-in.com wants to track the user journey from the online experience to the in-store experience and back and update all other data points (other tools). The detail needed here is field-level/click-level tracking. This should be completed in addition to GA3/GA4 transition.
2. Access and democratisation of data through both tactical and strategic dashboarding and reports that provide valuable and timely insights to the senior leadership team, Shoe-in.com customers, and internal teams.
3. Segmentation – Shoe-in.com wants to be able to look across all product lines and understand and segment the difference in user behaviour based on key variables defined in the Measurement Plan and Metric and Dimension Library.
4. Governance, Process, and Data Accuracy. Continue governance and documentation on existing implementation. Several documents have been created, but broader use and acceptance are needed.

There needs to be a transparent and standardised process for creating, making changes to, and notifying published changes to reports and an agreed plan for regular testing to ensure continued data accuracy.

What Problems Are We Trying To Solve?

Both external and internal teams have already completed a large amount of foundational work. From this, we can now more clearly define and understand the problems and opportunities this updated plan seeks to address.

At Shoe-in.com, we want to clearly understand the user experience of our product and services and provide valuable, timely, and personable communication and content to define audiences and segments.

Shoe-in.com are often busy and juggling priorities. This has often led to analytics work being deprioritised or postponed.

1. Prioritisation and Scope – this needs to be clearly defined. There are lots of personalisation strategies; which are best for Shoe-in.com?
2. Governance, Documentation, and Process – how do we maintain what we've created and enable a process of continuous improvement based on sound foundations?
3. POS Project – is complete. Slow progress here has hindered other areas, such as establishing a Federated ID.
4. Re-work of the initial CDP implementation is required to integrate with the CRM system.
5. Working in Silos – various external and internal teams are working in silos. Cross-channel collaboration is required to communicate with customers across the entire customer journey.

We estimate Shoe-in.com to be at level 3 on the Analytics Maturity Curve. Still, with a sufficient lack of governance and reporting, they could also be considered at level 1 and level 2 in some areas. We aim to reach level 4 in 12 months by addressing some of the critical strategic improvement areas above.

Principles

These will guide our discussion and planning, but most importantly, our decision-making. Each option should be weighed against our principles to increase the likelihood that it's aligned with our overall strategy.

- We don't cut corners, and we do things right the first time
- We work as a team to a set plan
- NEVER leave data interpretation to the executives
- Start with the end in mind
- Data is a shared asset

These principles must be defined in collaboration with Shoe-in.com. They will help us address decisions such as the recent Federated ID question. An example of a principle might be 'to do it right the first time' or agree that an audience must be entirely usable throughout the network of tools and teams before being deemed complete.

We must also understand exactly what assets will be included in this work for implementation. Below is an example of web assets, like websites/applications or iframes – anything that could be cobbled together to create the online user journey. For large organisations, it's not unusual to have a Frankenstein's monster implementation with user journeys stitched across different technology subdomains, subfolders, and root domains. Unfortunately, you need a Frankenstein solution to match if that's the case.

Web Assets In Scope

In scope	Notes
Digital Assets	
• **Marketing Website:** Shoe-in.com • **Marketing Website:** Shoe-in.co.uk • **Product/Application (Product Design):** Shoe-in.design.com • **Product/Application (Customer Portal):** Shoe-in/portal.com	All other digital assets are not listed as in scope. We understand that the work done for the desktop will also work for mobile. In future, there will be a mobile app. Assuming local sites are on subdomains.
Out-of-Scope Digital Assets	
1. **Other:** • Landing pages • Payment gateways • iFrames • Corporate website • Customsocks.com	We recommend revisiting these assets at some point, as well as the other GA3 properties listed in the shoe-in.com Google Analytics Account. Note if there are any possible unknown landing pages, payment gateways, or iFrames. Additional brands and sites, like customsocks.com, are not included in this project scope.

Once we know where we're implementing, we need to know the level of detail. How much resolution do we need now and later? This could be different for different stages in the customer journey.

In our example, Tier 3 is the highest level with most data

points captured in the User Journey, while Tier 1 is just the data captured on a page load, with no custom event tracking included.

Tier Target Per Asset

There are three key tiers defined in shoe-in.com website analytics. Please refer to the definitions below.

Tier	Definition	Equivalent to
1 Page (load)	Page load events and variables	Page tracking
2 CTA & CJM*	Clicks on Call-to-action buttons like Next or Join Now Clicks on Customer Journey milestones like Login	Interaction tracking & partial engagement tracking
3 Fields & Clicks	All user-clickable fields	Full engagement tracking

*Customer Journey milestones.

Each asset will be completed to a certain tier level with an associated telemetry coverage (as a percentage). Please see the Solution Design (Section 6.3) for more information on the tiers and the Measurement Plan for detailed examples.

Digital Assets	2022 Progress	Target Tier
Marketing Website: 1. Shoe-in.com	Tier 1–2 most CTA's and CJM's in place but need testing.	Tier 2. Finish implementation.
Marketing Website: 2. Shoe-in.co.uk	Tier 1*. No CTA's or CJM.	Tier 2. These top-of-funnel interactions are needed for future audience targeting.

Product/ Application 1. Shoe-in.design.com	Tier 1*.	Tier 3. Important for optimising shoe design application and experience.
Product/ Application 2. Shoe-in/ portal.com	Tier 1*.	Tier 3. Necessary for collecting detailed audience preferences (logged-in).

*GA4 is not set up through CPD. Auto-events in GA4 and no conversion tracking.

Once we have identified the level of detail required, we can start planning with our developers, other teams, and stakeholders how to break the necessary work items into projects and phases and when those projects and phases should take place. Some projects can run in parallel with multiple teams, but some projects or phases will require a critical path of steps where one must take place before another.

This is the order and the dates we are looking to work through for each asset and tool. The timeline is adaptable based on developer availability and any additional work needed, considering Shoe-in.com's specific requirements for the implementation.

Some information will need to be worked out as you go, so it is important to keep revisiting and updating the project plan. Ideally, all details can be fleshed out before starting. Still, it's rare for companies to have sufficient visibility and resources to do this without an initial business case, which the project plan aims to provide.

When assessing whom we might need in our team, we can again look at the possible roles to determine their project requirements. As discussed in the 'Jack-of-All-Trades' subchapter, for small companies some of these roles must be combined.

Something like a RACI Matrix (See Appendix 1) would be

recommended for any large project; it shows the possible tasks involved in a project and a breakdown between different roles: Project Sponsor, Business Analyst, Head of Analytics, Web Analytics Specialist, Project Manager, Marketing Manager, and Web Developer.

Key Projects

The following outlines the key projects required at each stage of the Solution Design with estimated work in hours. Projects will be phased in the project roadmap based on priorities and capacity to meet the key personalisation strategies (for a full worked example, see Appendix 2).

Projects by Stage and Type of Work	Detail	Target Start	Estimated Hours
IMPLEMENTATION			
CONNECTIONS			
REPORTING AND DASHBOARDING			
MARTECH INTEGRATIONS			
BACK-END AND OFFLINE INTEGRATIONS			
PREDICTION AND PERSONALISATION			
TESTING			
TRAINING AND WORKSHOPS			

Delivery And Costing

Potential Resourcing Requirements:

Our examples here suggest involvement from a specialist internal team or support from an external agency or consultancy.

Several variables will affect the level of resourcing required for a project like this:

- The existing specialised skillset within the team and knowledge of exact requirements
- Availability of time from developers, marketers, and other stakeholders
- The complexity of the website structure and the number of assets
- The number of tools
- Time by which the project should be completed

Based on the current scope and previous intensity level, we recommend a monthly budget of 60 hours of focused resources for the next 12 months. This would also require investment from the shoe-in.com team specifically to assist in engagement field-level tracking, other projects, and further modifications per the analytics library.

Estimated breakdown of hours, assuming internal strategic support (to be defined in Communications Plan):

- Head of Analytics – 3 hours
- Project Management – 10 hours
- Insights and Reporting Specialist – 10 hours
- Web Analytics Specialist – 15 hours
- Product Owners – 10 hours
- Developers – 10 hours

Estimated Budget:

Sixty hours. Budgeted cost based on varying rates.

Time and budget will be broken out and agreed upon in detail in monthly Strategic Meetings (see Appendix 3 for the full Communication Plan).

6.3 – SOLUTION DESIGNS – BIRDSEYE VIEW

The Solution Design is a working document to be updated as we go. It goes into further detail and is used by the implementation and data teams to understand the structure and reasoning behind the overall solution.

Like the project plan, the level of complexity for a solution design will be determined by the scale and complexity of your project. Larger organisations may even need to hire a Solutions Architect to create detailed drawings of all the tools in the stack and the various stages of data flow between the multiple pieces of hardware and software. A solution design for the Analytics Maturity Curve can also be drafted in phases. To break up the task, we might decide to create a simple solution design with very few connections for our planned move from level 1 to level 3 but then have separate future drafts for our setup for the much more complex and challenging levels 4 and 5.

Here is a simple and effective visualisation from Ruben Ugarte, author of *Bulletproof Decisions.* He argues that our marketing stacks should be modular, where we focus on choosing tools that are 'good enough' for now, without worrying whether we will be able to scale with a specific vendor or getting locked into solutions that end up not working as promised. More on this in Let's Go Tool Shopping – Chapter 8.

A basic solution design could look like this, in this case using Segment as the CDP of choice:

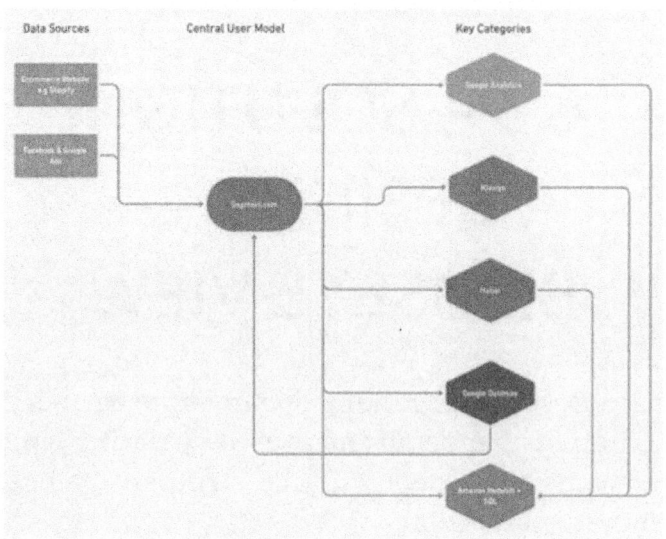

Source: https://rubenugarte.com/marketing-stack/

Continuing our shoe-in.com example, our solution could look like this:

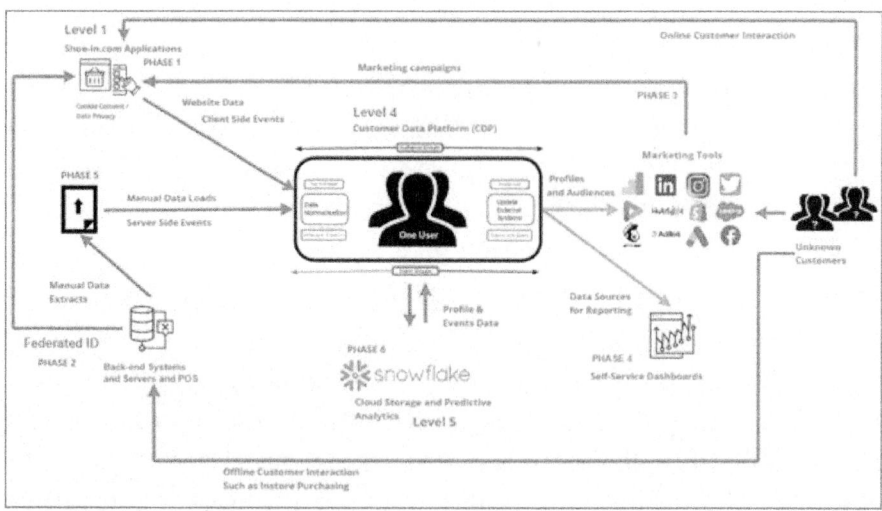

Source: MckTui Consulting.

6.3 – SOLUTION DESIGNS – BIRDSEYE VIEW

We can plan out our project phases, at least initially, in a simple table. In this example, I've also noted at what points we would have hoped to have levelled up, once everything needed for that level is in place (for a full breakdown for the stages and phases, please see Appendix 4).

Customer Touchpoint Planning

We can also plan our implementation by focusing on who our customers are and visualising what information we intend to collect (with permission) and when. This can allow us also to plan our value exchange, offering more and more personalisation in exchange for the additive data required to provide the additional service or product.

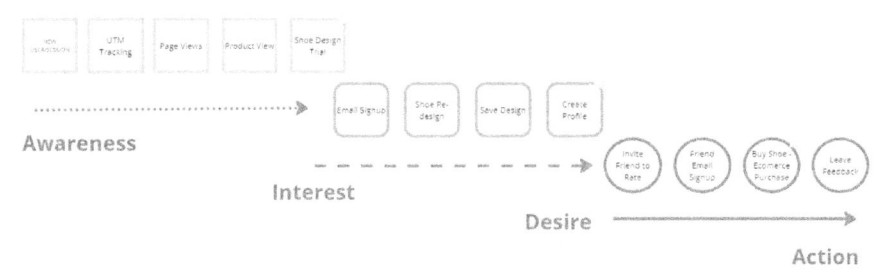

Source: MckTui Consulting.

6.4 – MEASUREMENT PLANS – THE MISSING

One thing that exasperates me more than anything else is companies' reluctance to create documents on how their website or app flows in steps and then specifically record what and how those steps are measured; some companies even outsource all that thinking and understanding to agencies. If you take anything from this book, ensure you have a regularly maintained and updated measurement plan to go along with your site and ensure that internal and external teams can always access it. If someone says the tracking is broken, expect a line-specific definition.

Marketer One – 'You know old line 33 on the sheet is broken again; it says here our agency fixed that only last week!'. Shocked response From Marketer Two – 'That's important because it triggers one of our key conversion goals. STFD! (shut the front door). Let's get on that!'

This document details what needs to be tracked as a checklist. Developers work through and update their comments, while the analytics team tests and assists developers.

But what should we have in our Measurement Plan, and how do we create and fill it in?

Here is a structure I recommend, using Google Sheets and breaking the sections into tabs.

- Overview – Audiences, Objectives, and Assets
- Conversions and Targets – Web Analytics (usually GA3 and

GA4)
- Event and DataLayer Tracking – This could be simple or detailed
- Configuration Checklist – Web Analytics (usually GA3 and GA4)
- UTM Link Tagging Tool

Overview – Audiences, Objectives, And Assets

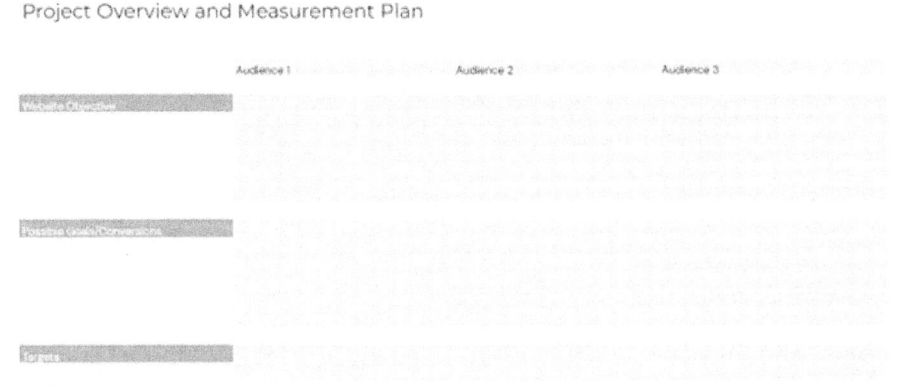

Project Overview and Measurement Plan

	Audience 1	Audience 2	Audience 3
Website Objective			
Possible Goals/Conversions			
Events			

Source: MckTui Consulting.

We start here with our website or app up on one screen and this sheet up on another. Who are the key audiences for assets? What do we want each audience to do? And what possible goals and events may be needed to track those specific engagements? Can we think of rough targets, such as the number of contact forms? How many assets (websites and apps) are we looking to track? And how can we start mapping out the potential properties and data streams we need? This would be required for setting up Google Analytics 4 if we decided that's the web analytics tool for us.

Conversions And Targets – Web Analytics (Usually Ga3 And Ga4)

	Audience	Website Objective	Conversion Va KPI	Target
App/Website Goals, URL:				
Macro Goal Action				
Required – Track 2				
Micro Action showing Desire				

Goal Name (Existing)	Conversions	Conditions	Measurement details	Status	Date Tested	In Scope?

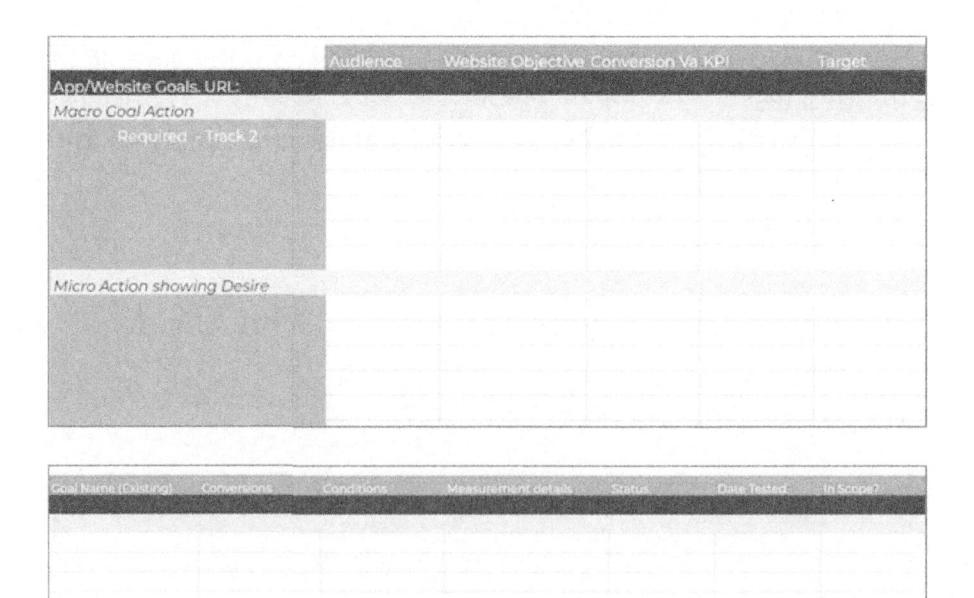

Source: McKtui Consulting.

Once we have a rough idea of those objectives and goals, we can break them into specific conversions. I find it helpful to map the most important and work my way down. Often these are bottom-of-the-funnel conversions as well. As many organisations will previously have had Google Analytics 3, this can also help to ensure we're transitioning our new setup based on the learnings and structure of the old. We can also note here particular conditions used to trigger our conversions; this is useful when we're unsure precisely what the data we're looking at really means.

Event And Datalayer Tracking – This Could Be Simple Or Detailed

Event Name	Parameter Name - 1	Parameter 1 - Value	PN2	PV2	PN3	PV3	PN4	PV4	PN5	PV5	Trigger
URL - Shoe-in.com											
Custom Events	These are custom to you but based on the recommended name and structure for GA4 events										
Required - Track 2											
Recommended Events	All these events are the recommended naming and structure for GA4 events										
Enhanced Measurement	All these events are tracked automatically by enhanced measurement of GA4										

Source: MckTui Consulting.

Once we have our agreed conversions, we can break down the engagements that we want to track, identifying those as events and the parameters we may wish to pass on with those events. The best way to start here is by noting those events already tracked in the tool and those recommended, following the tool's existing structure, before attempting any original custom tracking.

In order to effectively manage and analyse data in web analytics, it is important to standardise the data points across different setups and libraries. By doing this, you ensure that the data you collect is consistent and compatible across various uses. Standardisation helps streamline processes and improve the quality of your data. It also enables you to analyse and compare data more effectively. So, when setting up your data layer and working with different data libraries, make sure to define a set of standardised data points that are relevant to each type of engagement. This will help you maintain consistency and get the most out of your web analytics efforts.

6.5 – CODE, METRICS, AND DIMENSION LIBRARIES

Just as important as agreeing on what to track is agreeing and documenting exactly how to track. To solve the skills gap between marketers and developers, we must have agreed, revised, and reusable libraries. Where the project plan documents precisely what we should do, and when the solution design gives us the step-back bird's eye view, the measurement defines the detail of what should be tracked. Libraries like this example ensure good governance and define the how of what we should do because, like most things, there are many ways to skin a cat.

dataLayer and Variable Planning for Events

WHO	Custom Variable 1	Variable 2	Variable 3	Variable 4	Variable 5
	Cookie ID (Default)	Company ID	User ID	Federated ID	POS ID

	Variable 5	Variable 6	Variable 7	Variable 8	Variable 9
WHERE	Page Section	Site Section	Product Category		
	Header	Awareness	Running		
	Body	Interest	Climbing		
	Footer	Desire	Walking		
		Action	Lounge Wear		
		Payment Pages			

	Variable 9	Variable 10	Variable 11	Variable 12	Variable 13
WHAT	Unique ID	State Change	Event Type	Group	Event Label
	Element ID	Checked	Button	Interaction	Check box
		Unchecked	Text Field	Show	Success
		Focused	Selections	Click	Radio
		Unfocused	Login	Systems set	Dropdown
			Promotions		Text input
			Products		Submit
			Link		CTA
			Error		

Source: MckTui Consulting.

Our Excel sheet shows all the variables and the possible data passed into those variables for each page section and site section, our example being the online store shoe-in.com. By working through this ahead of time, we can be sure that the data we need will be available when we need it. Any of these data points could help us build up our picture of the customer. We could stagger the collection in our customer touch point planning and look to build our collection over time. Still, we'll need a detailed plan of the data we want to collect to build a good picture of our customers, our website performance, and our marketing and to enable higher-curve activities and greater personalisation.

What Is A Datalayer

We often call this a data layer or *dataLayer*. A dataLayer is a standardised way of organising and storing data on a website.

It's a JavaScript object that sits on a website's back-end and is used to collect and store information about user behaviour and interactions on the website.

In essence, a dataLayer acts as a bridge between a website's front-end and back-end, making it easier for marketers to access and analyse important data. It allows marketers to easily collect information such as page views, button clicks, form submissions, and other user interactions. It's most often associated with client-side tracking but can be adapted for server-side tracking as well. What is most important is the agreed list of variables to pass at customer touchpoint or stage of the customer journey.

Once created, you can work with your developer to create a template for each important page, site, or app section that sets the expectation of what data should be passed in the dataLayer and when. This could be the dataLayer initialised by Google Tag Manager or coded for a CDP, but ideally, we should work to a point where we create own our own dataLayer or list of ready-to-access data points, ready, of course, for Server-side or Client-side tracking.

6.5 – CODE, METRICS, AND DIMENSION LIBRARIES

```
<script>
  dataLayer = [{
    'ecommerce': {
      'purchase': {
        'actionField': {
          'id': '12345',              // Transaction ID. Required fo
          'affiliation': 'Online Store',
          'revenue': '54.99',         // Total transaction value (in
          'tax': '4.99',
          'shipping': '5.00'
        },
        'products': [{                // List of productFieldObject
          'name': 'Men\'s Running Shoes', // Name or ID is required.
          'id': '1234',
          'price': '44.99',
          'brand': 'Nike',
          'category': 'Shoes',
          'variant': 'Red',
          'quantity': 1
        }]
      }
    }
  }];
</script>
```
Source: Chat GPT.

This allows us to standardise our own collection of data, independent of the tools we use and their eventual source, and build this requirement into the creation of any new page or application.

In this example, the dataLayer is set up to track an e-commerce purchase event for a pair of men's running shoes. The dataLayer includes information about the transaction (such as the transaction ID, revenue, tax, and shipping), as well as information about the product itself (such as the product name, ID, price, brand, category, variant, and quantity).

A custom dataLayer could include additional information specific to the online shoe shop, such as the user's location, device type, referral source, and more. This data could be used to optimise the user experience, target marketing campaigns, and improve overall business performance.

Next, we're going to delve deeper into picking the right business and marketing strategy, which should ultimately guide our plans but is often missing in action.

◆ ◆ ◆

That was the bump, and we covered a lot.

We looked at a Measurement Plan, Solution Designs, Code, Metrics, and Dimensions Libraries.

We even looked at categorising your web analytics implementation with tiers. Take what you need. Use what you can and know the level of detail and governance planning you could be working to, and if your data keeps getting F**ked, what level you will need to work towards.

In the upcoming chapter, we'll select our **Personalisation Strategy** and confront the risks and opportunity costs of inaction.

In this chapter, we will make decisive choices. Get ready to embark on a limitless journey of personalisation and unlock the path to growth.

References And Bibliography

1. Ugarte, R. (n.d.). The Marketing Stack: A Guide to Essential Marketing Tools. Retrieved from https://rubenugarte.com/marketing-stack/
2. Montgomery, D. J., & Jackson, G. W. (1995). Managing the project team: A performance-based approach. Project Management Journal, 26(1), 25-32.

CHAPTER 7 – PICKING A STRATEGY

Discover the Marketing Stack in this chapter, shaping the value we place on our marketing, content, and analytics. We dig into Google's $85 million settlement in Arizona, highlighting the significance of legal compliance.

We look at how you can conduct your own **Risk and Readiness Review**, understand which areas are your weakest and strongest, where your risks lie, and a solid method for choosing the right personalisation strategy for your organisation on the **Wheel of Growth**.

Get ready to unlock valuable insights and propel your marketing efforts forward.

7.1 – IT COMES FROM THE TOP – OR NOT

The biggest, most consistent problem I've found is when an organisation does not have SMART business strategies supporting SMART marketing strategies informing and guiding digital marketing strategies. Or they exist but are not communicated or, for some reason, do not guide the company's day-to-day running.

What are SMART targets again, and why is it important?

SMART goals and targets are a popular framework for setting objectives that are specific, measurable, achievable, relevant, and time-bound. The acronym SMART stands for:

Specific: The goal or target should be well-defined and focused. It should answer the questions of who, what, where, when, and why.

Measurable: The goal or target should be quantifiable so that progress can be tracked and evaluated. It should answer the questions of how much, how many, or how often.

Achievable: The goal or target should be realistic and attainable, given the resources and constraints available.

Relevant: The goal or target should be relevant and aligned with the broader objectives or mission.

Time-bound: The goal or target should have a specific deadline or timeline for completion.

7.1 – IT COMES FROM THE TOP – OR NOT

Examples of SMART goals and targets might include increasing sales revenue by 10% in the next quarter, reducing customer wait times by 20% within the next six months, or launching a new product line by the end of the year.

The bigger the company, the more this is prevalent; a big company is like a big tanker. It takes more time and more people working together (or not) to gradually move it one way or another. Working alongside, or sometimes within, these organisations can feel like pulling aside a big ship. The crew are waving their hands, shouting out of the portholes, asking you where the icebergs are, where they should go, and how to avoid them. Your first thought might be, why are you asking me? I can help you, but I can't tell you where you should be going.

Even if we can come up with the perfect direction, if it doesn't come from them, they won't believe it, and if the captain or captains do not fully endorse it, then it's all pointless. This point is particularly relevant to data and analytics. The state of the analytics is just one symptom of a bigger problem – a lack of leadership and strategic direction.

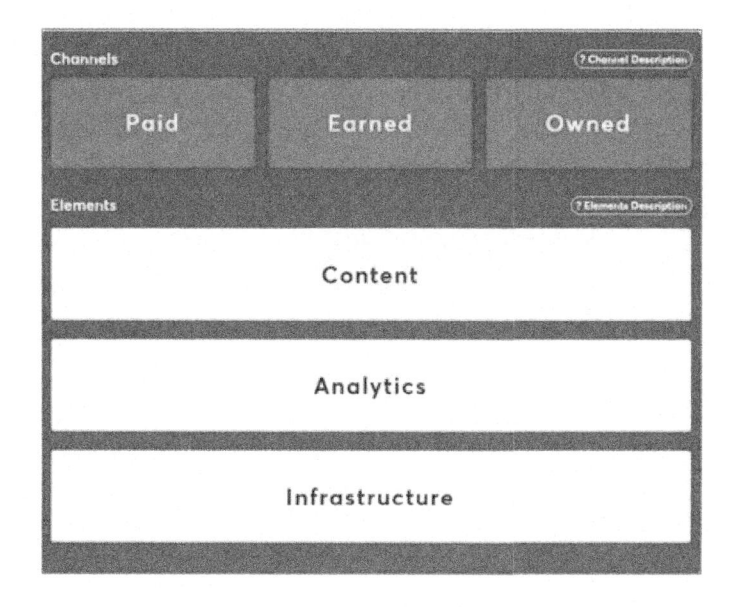

Channels		? Channel Description
Paid	Earned	Owned

Elements	? Elements Description
Content	
Analytics	
Infrastructure	

Source: Ian Luries 'Marketing Stack'.

Ian Luries has created an elegant, simple way to prioritise marketing activities following the structure of a typical sales funnel (see figure). The Marketing Stack shows the raw elements of marketing, breaking down types of marketing into the common paid, earned, and owned channels. Marketers and senior stakeholders often think from the top down. They're considering where to spend advertising dollars and what the website or content looks like. However, while Analytics and Infrastructure come last, they are the most important: they are the foundations of everything but often receive the least investment or attention as part of the marketing and business strategy.

You could spend a million dollars on your campaign, and it may deliver awareness, sales, or leads, but if you don't have the working infrastructure, you can't process payments. If you don't have operational analytics, you might not know what worked and what didn't and so you can't learn, and you can't recreate your previous success and avoid the failures.

I know of a massive e-commerce website that is guilty of this – a vast international retail shopping chain. Post-COVID, they were unsure what to do about online. Customers wanted online shopping, but for them, it was far less profitable to encourage their customers to purchase online; for years, they were behind the times in everything digital. Their analytics was broken and had been for at least 12 months. It regularly reported only half of what was sold online. This fed into all their paid, earned, and owned marketing, leaving them potentially wasting thousands monthly on ineffective marketing or unreported infrastructure and UX content issues. Still, like Blockbuster before Netflix, no one wanted to acknowledge what was happening before it was too late. Those working within the company received very little support from the top and regularly left when realising how pointless and ineffective their role was without support.

An excellent place to start is to assess this for yourself:
- Is your business more focused on **effectiveness** or **efficiency** at scale?
- For example, is your team focused on driving better **ROI** or overall **user experience**?
- What proportion of your sales and operations are **offline** vs. **online**?
- Are you looking for greater **acquisition and growth** or **customer loyalty and retention**?
- Is your aspiration to offer **innovative** products and services, or are you more **conservative** and more comfortable working with proven ideas or technologies?

What makes your organisation great, and what do you want to improve? How is your company strategically positioned? Are you a Walmart or a Tesla? That must be clearly and widely known before thinking about personalisation strategies. One of the key reasons for this is that without an agreed direction throughout the company, you will achieve no traction. Good data requires everyone within the organisation to see why good data is a fundamental part of your direction and should be financially and strategically supported. More often than not, data is stored in silo tools and teams; those teams have seemingly competing priorities.

7.2 – OPPORTUNITY COST

It is OK not to do anything, to actively decide not to work towards predictive analytics, or even that omni-channel marketing is not worthwhile for your organisation. Still, that decision should be regularly balanced against the potential opportunity cost. However, to effectively balance that decision, your organisation will need to be at least level 2 on the Analytics Maturity Curve, or you won't have the necessary insight to make an informed decision. Making no decision is still making a decision, and it's risky to be out there churning around and around in circles. Eventually, you will run out of fuel.

7.3 – RISK

Some organisations are naturally more risk-averse than others. Whether we understand this area of digital marketing or not, it is increasingly presenting more and more of a risk to the organisations we work for. The law is not set on this subject and continues evolving alongside the various political, economic, social, and technological factors.

NetDoktor, a medical website in Austria, operates similarly to countless others on the internet. When a user visits the website, a Google Analytics cookie is placed on their device, which tracks their activity during their visit. This tracking includes the pages visited, the duration of the visit, and device information. Additionally, Google assigns a unique identification number to the user's browser, which can potentially be linked with other data.

NetDoktor can leverage this analytics data to gain insights into its readership and their interests, with the website having control over the specific data it chooses to collect. However, since Google Analytics is utilised for traffic monitoring, all data collected is routed through Google's servers and ultimately ends up in the United States. This transfer of personal data across the Atlantic can present challenges for data regulators in Europe.

NetDoktor unwittingly found itself at the centre of an almighty tussle between US laws and Europe's strict privacy regulations.

On December 22, the Austrian data regulator, Datenschutzbehörde, said that 'The use of Google Analytics on NetDoktor breached the European Union's General Data Protection Regulation (GDPR)'. The data being sent to the US wasn't properly protected against potential access by US intelligence agencies. Incredulously it was later decided that the European Parliament's COVID-19 testing website had also breached GDPR by using cookies from Google Analytics and Stripe, according to a European Data Protection Supervisor (EDPS) decision.

This is all moving so quickly that the right hand doesn't know what the left hand is doing. As responsible marketers, we need to be aware of this potential threat and raise it where we find it.

The two cases are the first decisions following a July 2020 ruling that Privacy Shield, the mechanism used by thousands of companies to move data from the EU to the US, was illegal. These landmark cases will probably pile pressure on negotiators in the US and Europe who are trying to replace Privacy Shield with a new way for data to flow between the two. If an agreement takes too long, similar cases across Europe could have a domino effect, with cloud services from Amazon, Facebook, Google, and Microsoft all potentially being ruled incompatible, one country at a time. 'This is an issue that touches all aspects of the economy, all aspects of social life,' says Gabriela Zanfir-Fortuna, Vice President of Global Privacy at Future of Privacy Forum, a nonprofit think tank.

NetDoktor isn't unique, but the case clearly conveys that European regulators still don't like how US tech companies send data across the Atlantic.

NetDoktor should have anticipated the shifting sands around them and the potential threat of putting a seemingly inconspicuous and widely used tracking cookie on their website. After all, according to Google, their technology is supposedly first party, so considerations like this are less important. This ignores completely that for NetDoktor's customers, Google is at the very least a second unknown actor, and whatever party it is, European citizens' data is being stored and processed in American servers.

You would have thought that Google itself would protect their users and customers from such a potentially costly mistake, but a recent case shows that even they are at risk here from litigation, too and are finding their own footing. A recent lawsuit filed by the State of Arizona alleged that Google collected location data even after users opted out of tracking.

Google parent company Alphabet Inc. will pay $85 million to end a consumer privacy lawsuit filed by the state of Arizona. The suit, filed in May 2020, alleged that the search engine violated the state's Consumer Fraud Act and misled internet users about using location data and data collection practices. It accused Google of tracking user location without consent to increase ad revenue, even after users had turned off location history in settings.

Arizona Attorney General Mark Brnovich's office began investigating Google's location data collection practices following a 2018 Associated Press story that revealed how the search engine company tracks user movements.

'When I was elected Attorney General, I promised Arizonans I would fight for them and hold everyone, including corporations like Google, accountable', Brnovich said in a press release. 'I am proud of this historic settlement that proves no entity, not even big tech companies, is above the law.'

Get your teams together and work through some initial questions. You will need to make sure the answers are as accurate as possible. Depending on your organisation, the geographic location of your customers, and your appetite for risk, the next best step may be to contact your lawyer for final confirmation.

- We have a good understanding of what this means and how it might affect my organisation?
- Do we rely on third-party cookies for ad-retargeting/

- programmatic cross-site tracking or other uses?
- Do we think this will significantly affect how we market and sell to our customers?
- Is data privacy and big concern in our market field?
- How do we currently manage permission and consent?

The cases in Arizona and Austria show that collecting and using personal data can now bring a high financial cost. In Chapter 1, we discussed the importance of audits. Google Analytics, by default, will record any information that is stored in a web page URL. Developers often transfer customer information from one web asset to another by keeping the information in the URL. Don't get caught out with PII accidentally stored in your Google Analytics property or data stream; be aware that without regular audits and governance, you may not be following the proper guidelines.

In The Pillars of Personalisation – Chapter 5 – we reviewed the pillars required for effective personalisation. We primarily concerned ourselves with our strengths and potential opportunities. Let's look at the possible risks using the same Risk and Readiness Review framework.

As part of your Risk and Readiness Review, along with the questions and statements above, you should explore these key areas – this time rating a high score for a threat and a low score if we don't perceive this as an issue.

Risk Assessment – Threats

3rd Party Reliance				
Google Display Network/Double Click				
Programmatic				
DMP				
Mobile Ads				
Display Retargeting				
2nd Party Reliance				

Source: MckTui Consulting.

Just like before, we can collect our key findings in an overall score and look to summarise those findings for senior decision-makers and the rest of the organisation.

> **"The price of light is less than the cost of darkness."**
>
> — Arthur Nielsen, Founder of Nielsen

Opportunity Cost
- Customers expect greater personalisation. That could be more relevant and timely communication or a tailored on-site experience with personalised recommendations.
- Digital marketers are expected to nail the 4 P's in real-time.

Privacy and Consent
- Customers expect brands to know them and provide personalised services and recommendations while simultaneously respecting their privacy.

Third- and Second-Party Over-Reliance
- Cross-channel and cross-device tracking is less effective than previously. A third party can no longer track a user across domains using a cookie.

Data Security

Manage the trade-off with a solid first-party data strategy or disappoint customers and see the effectiveness and efficiency of existing marketing ebb away.

Here is an example of a potential output from this exercise:

Your Score Card - Risks

Risk and Readiness Review – Led by a Web Analytics Specialist, this aims to quantify the organizations readiness and risks. We look at possible opportunities and threats across four key areas: Data as Resource, Tools and the MarTech Stack, Analytics Maturity and Risk.

Key Risks

- Risk at 60% - Relatively high.
  - Potential exposure using 3rd party tools and Bad PR from any resulting breach.
  - Ambiguity around privacy and consent management and lack of permissions.
  - Moderate exposure to 3rd party and 2nd party reliance.

Score Card

Potential Risk   60%

Just like in 'Pillars of Personalisation', we go through our Risk and Readiness Review, mark down our scores, and compute a percentage out of 100.

7.4 – THE WHEEL OF GROWTH

Once we have done a bit of self-reflection on our readiness and appetite for risk, reviewed our business-level and marketing strategies, set clear targets and KPIs, and worked through the three pillars of personalisation, the fun part can begin. We can start thinking about the most effective personalisation strategies for our business and decide our best route to growth.

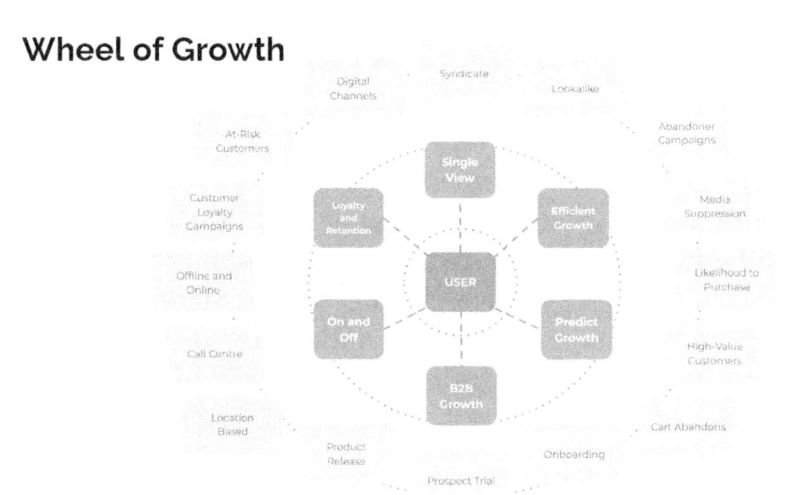

Wheel of Growth

Source: MckTui Consulting.

Some strategies are better for driving effectiveness and some for efficiency; some focus on the user experience, and others on efficient growth. Are we interested in online, or is the integration of offline data where we see our next opportunity?

Are we looking for market growth or loyalty? Do we see ourselves as early or late adopters of technology, or can these strategic questions be narrowed down to help us choose the most appropriate strategy?

Building A Single Customer View

This would typically be the first syndication across all our customer touchpoints, and then we would use that syndication, often through a Federated ID, to ensure a consistent message across all our digital channels. Our first case study in Chapter 1 (Wickes Boosts Shopper Engagement) is an excellent example..

Once we have a single view of a customer, we can ensure privacy and honour our customer's privacy preferences. See the further example on KMART.

Developing Customer Loyalty And Retention Strategies That Keep Buyers Coming Back

Sometimes the best growth comes from holding market share, or market or product development. We can start retaining our customers better by identifying those at risk. We can seek to understand what types of interactions indicate that customers are unhappy with our services. Some of this data could be collected from NPS scoring, or we could look for indicative interactions, such as a customer regularly seeking assistance from help pages; we can even mine information from call centres.

Once we have identified and tracked these potentially negative and positive interactions, we can compute them into a score. A great existing framework for this is the HEART framework, which is a set of user-centric metrics. It was developed to evaluate the quality of the user experience and help teams measure the impact of UX changes. As covered in Chapter 2, the framework is a kind of UX metrics scorecard breaking user experience down into five factors.

After reaching level 5, our next step might be to use these scores to predict whether a customer is unhappy using fewer data points or to fuel customer loyalty programmes by rewarding certain behaviours.

Creating Scalable And Efficient Customer Acquisition And Growth

In The Forgotten Role of the Marketer – Chapter 3 – we discussed the preposterous banana salesman harassing his customers and how we can and should do better. We can do that by showing the right type of advertising and messaging at the right time – tailoring and suppressing ads to ensure messaging is appropriate. Once we understand what works, we use those data points with walled gardens like Facebook and Google to find loosely matching audiences to expand our own.

To ensure this is sustainable, we must increase our ROI by increasing our CLV by steadily moving paid audiences into owned by earning their trust and repeat business.

Driving Omni-Channel Personalisation With Offline And Online Data

Recent Cannes winner Data Tienda showed us what could be achieved by personalising credit scores using offline and online data. Still, we could explore combining data from other key customer touchpoints like call centres and improving our marketing with additional offline data points such as their location.

Generating Predictive Insights And Customer Analytics That Drive Marketing Effectiveness

Of course, the sky is the limit here, and we can make sweeping predictions about anything or everything; the method can be complicated or not depending on what we decide to do, but a good place to start is by making predictions about whether or not our marketing will work when presented to a specific audience or segment. We can do this based on what we know about them so far, correlated with what we know about those who have or have not converted previously. We then create a predictive score and use that along with our paid bidding. If an audience is highly likely to convert, our prediction score should be higher, and we up the bids on that audience and any lookalike audiences already out there. If the score is lower, then we lower the bids.

7.5 – PERSONALISATION STRATEGY AND PROCESS

Let's pull it all together. Whichever personalisation strategy we choose, we must make sure it aligns with our overall business strategies – for example, whether ROI is more important than revenue or you're looking to focus on loyalty rather than growth. Perhaps you have lots of offline data points. Then it might be that a personalisation strategy around location-based marketing is the best option to work towards.

We can use a framework like the personalisation strategy matrix below to assess predictably and consistently which strategies may be most appropriate. Remember our self-question exercise at the start of this chapter? It is these answers that can guide us to the right personalisation strategy for our organisation.

By breaking the process down into these steps, we can begin to assemble our own strategies.

1. Self-Survey, Risk and Readiness Review – get all our stakeholders together, looking for gaps, opportunities, and threats across the three pillars.

2. Review our Marketing and Business Strategy.
3. Define our Data Strategy accordingly.
4. Review the Personalisation Strategy Matrix.
5. Summarise our Findings in the Nutshell. Keep it all to one page and in simple language.
6. Pick our Personalisation Strategies, layering these as we progress up the Analytics Maturity Curve.
7. Use our Actions Cards to start planning our approach.
8. Circle back to Plan, Plan, Plan to properly document our decisions and planning.

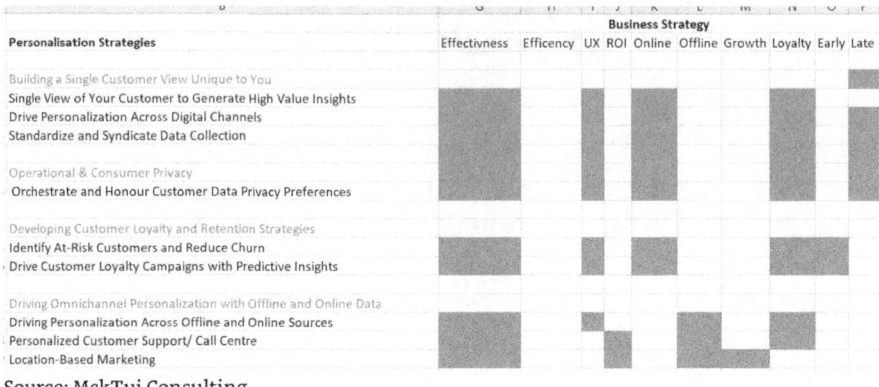

Personalisation Strategies	Effectivness	Efficency	UX	ROI	Online	Offline	Growth	Loyalty	Early	Late
Building a Single Customer View Unique to You										
Single View of Your Customer to Generate High Value Insights										
Drive Personalization Across Digital Channels										
Standardize and Syndicate Data Collection										
Operational & Consumer Privacy										
Orchestrate and Honour Customer Data Privacy Preferences										
Developing Customer Loyalty and Retention Strategies										
Identify At-Risk Customers and Reduce Churn										
Drive Customer Loyalty Campaigns with Predictive Insights										
Driving Omnichannel Personalization with Offline and Online Data										
Driving Personalization Across Offline and Online Sources										
Personalized Customer Support/ Call Centre										
Location-Based Marketing										

Source: MckTui Consulting.

It also often makes sense to start with some strategies over others. For example, the most logical starting point is to build a Single Customer View by standardising and syndicating data collection. Often as part of that strategy, the first attribute we want to collect is permission status – specifically, do we have permission to use this data or not?

7.5 – PERSONALISATION STRATEGY AND PROCESS

Single View

Single View of Your Customer to Generate High Value Insights

Use a **single customer view** to drive cross-channel personalisation **in order to** understand our Customer's needs across multiple touchpoints.

Limitations/Pain Points:
1. No consistent Unique ID. Limitations with existing tools.
2. No CDP.
3. Lacking Data Warehouse.

Single View

Drive Personalisation Across Digital Channels

Use a **single customer view** to drive cross-channel personalisation **in order to** deliver a consistent, relevant and timely customer experience.

Limitations/Pain Points:
1. Tools collecting and using existing data in silos so difficult to coordinate across channels.
2. No easily accessible and shared personas.

Single View

Orchestrate and Honour Customer Data Privacy Preferences

Build a **transparent, accessible and controllable data supply chain** on which data governance can be built to comply with local regulations **in order to** build trust with customers and reduce regulatory compliance risk.

Limitations/Pain Points:
1. Ambiguity around privacy and consent management for current toolset.

Source: MckTui Consulting.

We can see here how it's possible to layer personalisation strategies over time to meet a loftier overall marketing or business strategy. By doing this, we can make the task more achievable, breaking it down and supporting our organisation and other shipmates to come along for the ride. We can show how something potentially dull (even though we know it's not), like data privacy, is just a step to award-winning and profitable personalised omni-channel campaigns.

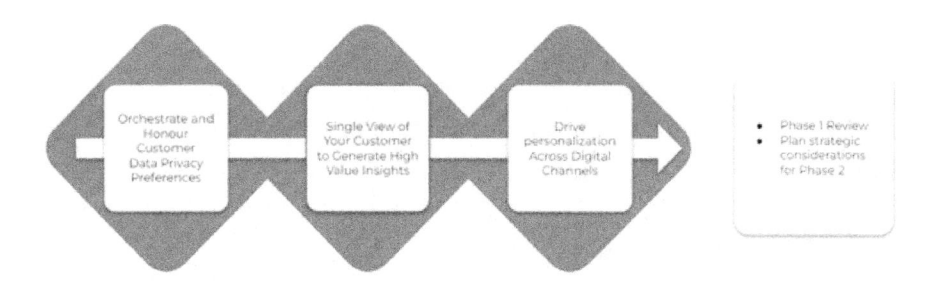

- Orchestrate and Honour Customer Data Privacy Preferences
- Single View of Your Customer to Generate High Value Insights
- Drive personalization Across Digital Channels
- Phase 1 Review
- Plan strategic considerations for Phase 2

Source: MckTui Consulting.

With hundreds of potential strategies, how do we decide on the best one to recommend for our organisation? A good way to start is to condense our information onto cards and attempt to summarise our findings in a nutshell, like the one below. This can help to focus our thinking.

Here are the results of our Risk and Readiness Review and how those results led us to a Data Strategy and Personalisation Strategy. What may also be helpful here, and could be included in our 'Nutshell', is how this relates to our overall marketing and business strategy.

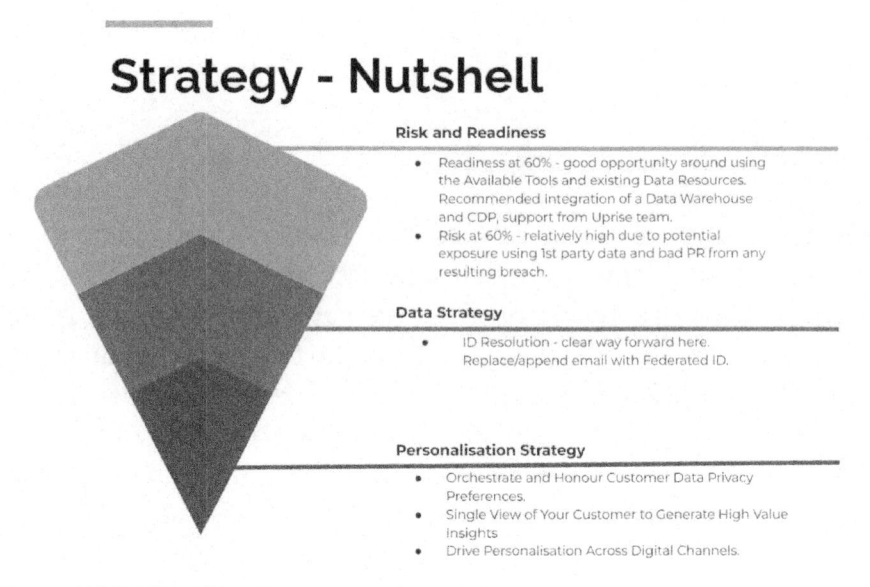

Strategy - Nutshell

Risk and Readiness
- Readiness at 60% - good opportunity around using the Available Tools and existing Data Resources. Recommended integration of a Data Warehouse and CDP, support from Uprise team.
- Risk at 60% - relatively high due to potential exposure using 1st party data and bad PR from any resulting breach.

Data Strategy
- ID Resolution - clear way forward here. Replace/append email with Federated ID.

Personalisation Strategy
- Orchestrate and Honour Customer Data Privacy Preferences.
- Single View of Your Customer to Generate High Value Insights
- Drive Personalisation Across Digital Channels.

Source: MckTui Consulting.

In a nutshell: By implementing a Federated ID across marketing touchpoints and linking to data preferences, we can de-risk shoe-in.com from accidental leaks or misuse of first-party data and use first-party data to drive better ROI through more relevant communications.

Introduction of a Data Warehouse and CDP for improved syndication of toolsets and data.

The next step could be to include offline data as part of the personalisation strategy.

When we have identified a personalisation strategy to work towards, we can summarise our plan into Audience Action

Cards. These cards can help focus our minds on what customer data points we have (these can be referred to as attributes) and what we need, how that data can be used to build personas, segments, or audiences (whichever terminology we're most comfortable with).

Once we have this, we can work forward across and then down the card and plan what tools our data is going to be sourced or extracted from and what possible destinations might be part of our overall Solution Design and MarTech Stack that our data will flow into. The data is our target audiences, their attributes and segments, and other key metrics and dimensions that we want to activate across our marketing campaigns.

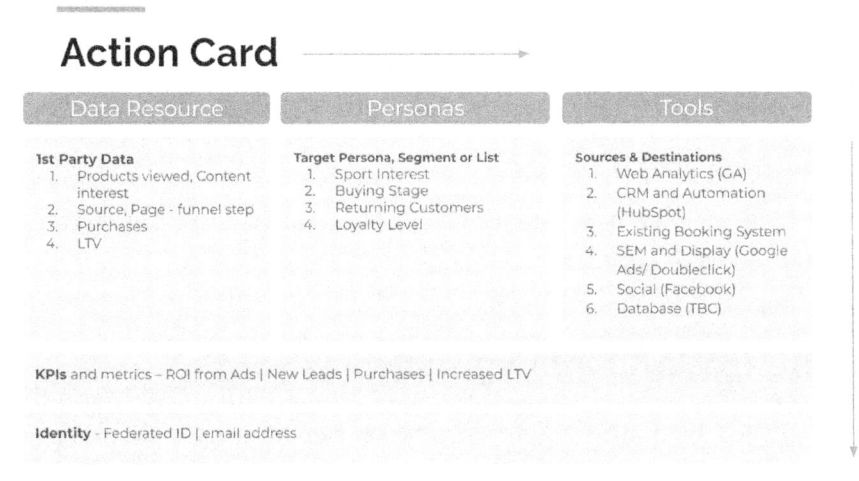

Action Card

Data Resource	Personas	Tools
1st Party Data 1. Products viewed, Content interest 2. Source, Page - funnel step 3. Purchases 4. LTV	**Target Persona, Segment or List** 1. Sport Interest 2. Buying Stage 3. Returning Customers 4. Loyalty Level	**Sources & Destinations** 1. Web Analytics (GA) 2. CRM and Automation (HubSpot) 3. Existing Booking System 4. SEM and Display (Google Ads/ Doubleclick) 5. Social (Facebook) 6. Database (TBC)

KPIs and metrics – ROI from Ads | New Leads | Purchases | Increased LTV

Identity - Federated ID | email address

Source: MckTui Consulting.

It is especially important to ensure we include our key performance indicators in this summary to show that those metrics are important and ensure that data is available. It is just as critical to think about all the potential identifiers and how they will be tied together in something like the previously mentioned Federated ID.

There may be a fair amount of work involved, but we now

have a structure to follow. It's only now that we have enough information to start looking at new tools and talking to outside vendors.

Depending on where you are with your journey, you may need to go back to your Solution Design to evaluate the necessary tools in your stack, or you may be able to proceed.

◆ ◆ ◆

Now you know what is on the line if the courts decide that your company or organisation has misused personal data.

We've added some additional frameworks to our kit and reviewed some of the most used Personalisation Strategies while reviewing what might be a most suitable fit for our Business and Marketing Strategy along with current progress and where we may need to improve.

Next, don't pass GO but collect two hundred pounds, and **Let's Go Tool Shopping** (Chapter 8).

What tools are we missing, and what must we consider in order to make good decisions?

References And Bibliography

1. Portent. (n.d.). One Trick to Set Strategic Goals Your Business Needs: Focus. [Blog post]. Retrieved from https://www.portent.com/onetrick/#setstrategicgoals
2. Tealium. (n.d.). The Joy of Data Cookbook. [White paper]. Retrieved from https://tealium.com/resource/whitepaper/the-joy-of-data-cookbook/
3. Rose, C. (2021). Acceleration Marketing in a World Without Third-Party Cookies [Blog post]. Retrieved from https://wtdotcom-prod.s3.amazonaws.com/assets/Acceleration_Marketing-in-a-world-without-

third-party-cookies-blog_Colleen-Rose_Jan202.pdf
4. Lomas, N. (2020). Google Analytics faces major GDPR compliance challenges in Europe. Wired UK. Retrieved from https://www.wired.co.uk/article/google-analytics-europe-austria-privacy-shield
5. Baker, W. (2021). Google Settles Consumer Privacy Lawsuit for $8.5 Million. Search Engine Journal. Retrieved from https://www.searchenginejournal.com/google-settles-consumer-privacy-lawsuit-for-85-million/466995/
6. Doran, G. T. (1981). There's a S.M.A.R.T. way to write management's goals and objectives. Management Review, 70(11), 35–36.

CHAPTER 8 – LET'S GO TOOL SHOPPING

Prepare for a no-nonsense exploration in this chapter as we critically examine SaaS sales pitches. It's time to ask the tough questions and make informed decisions about organising our tools and MarTech Stack.

We'll delve into the ongoing debate of investing in off-the-shelf tools versus developing custom in-house solutions. Is a **CRM system necessary for our business?** And what about data sovereignty? We'll uncover the implications of overlooking this critical consideration and how it can lead to financial ruin.

We navigate these **crucial considerations, empowering you to make strategic choices to enhance your MarTech Stack** and drive sustainable success. Get ready to challenge the status quo and optimise your tools for maximum effectiveness.

8.1 – THE PITCH

This is the most fun part of the process but also the most fraught with poor and lasting decisions. Most marketers don't want to be seen making the wrong decision, and it can be easy to get swept up in an exciting presentation that promises to deliver everything you need from your solution. This task is increasingly more complicated as SaaS products continue to grow and invest in continuous product development rather than refining their existing product and seeing their place as part of a modular stack and a broader ecosystem.

Source: craiyon.com – AI-generated image – 'A tech mastermind presenting an innovative product to corporate executives'.

It makes sense for them (like you) to work towards greater client lifetime value (CLV) and lock-in. They want to be able to offer you a one-stop shop and continue to sell and re-sell to you as your organisation grows. This can make their offering more complex, with inherent overlaps from one tool to another.

Have you sat through glossy tech presentations about new technologies like AI chatbots, CDPs, CRM systems or marketing automation tools that will change your business overnight? Have you sat puzzled when a salesperson sprouted the words 'turnkey solution' and privately recoiled when you realised they're comparing the software to turning the key in a car and driving away?

Here's the problem as I see it. What sells is the promise of an easy solution – that something NEW has come to the market and made all those problems of the past go away. It's often in an area of tech where the actual fundamentals of how the thing works just aren't easy enough to communicate honestly or excitingly in a one-hour presentation. So, the conversation is reduced to the bells and whistles and sometimes the charisma of the presenter – somebody with a lofty techy title and a list of paid-for awards (that's another subject).

I think there is always room for this, and we need to get excited about the possibilities of anything we're going to invest our time and money into, but there is a need for balance, and the goal here should not be just to get the sale and work it out later. For this reason, I'm a big fan of the consultative approach, and if you look closely and spot the patterns, you can see the difference.

In this example, I'm going to use a CDP (customer data platform). They are, to me, an obvious requirement for any company looking to scale effective personalisation and move past siloed marketing and communications and also avoid vendor lock-in.

When you collect your data in the same standardised format once (without multiple duplicate tags), things get a lot easier. With a CDP, you can consolidate the information and build audiences. These audiences can then be sent to each tool in your MarTech Stack, such as your CRM system, Facebook, Google Analytics, and AdWords. By doing this, successful conversions, events, and interactions will flow back and update those same audiences.

When it works, it's bloody brilliant, super effective, and delivers great results. You can further avoid lock-in to the CDP itself by having access to your own custom dataLayer and by only using the connections features within the tool.

Here's the problem. You can't and shouldn't get this to work in isolation from your current in-house capability (analytics maturity), existing MarTech Stack, and data resources (quantity and quality of usable data). The tool may be foolproof and perfect (never is), but it needs to fit into your existing business and stack, and if they are saying, 'don't worry, we'll take care of everything', do not touch it with a barge pole. I've seen this play out multiple times. You end up absolutely tied in and beholden to their magic system with no way for your own organisation to be able to develop and mature.

Before you start building a solution, you need to think strategically about what you want to achieve and what variables you need to consider. This will enable you to ask the right questions when presented with a shiny pitch. By doing so, you can ensure that you develop a solution that meets your specific needs and aligns with your business goals.

The cost will be an obvious component, but how will cost be structured over time, and how could it grow? What else do you need to consider? We can wrap the discussion up mostly into four overlapping key areas.

1. Custom Solutions versus Off-the-Shelf
2. Data Sovereignty
3. Total Real Cost
4. Considerations Per Tool

If you have not at least touched all these areas before bringing on a new tool, then you need more due diligence. Really all these points are about contingency planning for change. Your organisation's requirements, just like the world around us, are moving rapidly. What worked yesterday may not work tomorrow; you can't afford to be locked in.

8.2 – OFF-THE-SHELF OR OFF-TRACK

Should you buy MarTech tools off-the-shelf or look to build your own proprietary systems in-house? In most cases, you should be looking to build an integrated stack of off-the-shelf modular products and limit customisation as much as possible.

I remember hearing from a colleague that he had just come off a web call. He was excited and blown away by the call. He'd been talking to the Digital Analytics team. They had five specialists, all very good in their respective fields. The company sold a complicated monthly subscription service with long online forms and lots of competition, so a good online experience was paramount. To support this, the team had a radical plan for the enterprise –they were going to completely replace back-end systems, tag management systems, and web analytics tools with their own custom in-house solution. It promised to deliver everything you could ever want, and the team had already made a start.

Fast forward a year or two, and more sensible heads had prevailed. The new plan compromised with partial customisation of the data collection method (essentially, they could control and manage their own dataLayer) and a completely off-the-shelf stack, different to what was there previously but off-the-shelf nonetheless. Years down the line, the implementation is still in progress, and it will be for years to come, but they do have what they need right now.

Specialisation

In our highly competitive, interconnected world, to succeed in most endeavours now, you need to specialise. If you sell cars, get good at selling cars – not building a custom database because it has all the fields and features you want. If something is crucial to your project and your team has existing skills in that area, then try a small project building on that capability. However, know that their time will always be directed to the side project that only slightly enables the thing that you really want to be good at. You should also choose the best tool in your Solution Design for the job and for the Project Plan as a whole.

Integration And Modularity

You want a team of tools, not a family. Each tool must be a team player with other stacks. It must play nice with other tools, which means it needs to be able to connect and integrate easily through an API. I've lost count of the number of businesses I've worked with that are now burdened by legacy systems that don't connect to anything and are no longer being adequately supported. For this, have a CDP that does the connections piece. They specialise in creating and maintaining hundreds of API connections. Your team will be unable to maintain connections without a substantial ongoing investment.

It People Lock-In

Don't build an engine that only a few mechanics can work on. If you do, your company is entirely beholden to those mechanics, and if you do need more mechanics, it's going to be very difficult to find people who can work on your custom solution. Whether external or internal support, people must also be able to use what is in place. Is your interface really going to be better than that of a major SaaS provider with libraries of user guides and training? Do you want your organisation to be beholden to key people that become absolutely essential to running your entire infrastructure?

Vendor Lock-In

Just like we don't want to be locked into key people, we don't want to be completely locked into specific tools and vendors. If most of our stack comes from one provider, it could be costly to move on, and there can be a good reason to move on. What if they increase the cost of the tool? What if the tool's effectiveness falls behind the market because they stop investing in product development? What if the tool does not actually perform as you expected? What if the tool becomes illegal to use because it breaches privacy laws?

Crm Is Not The Solution

What really is a CRM system? It's a customer relationship management system where you hold and organise your customer's data. It's the modern example of those old Rolodexes that I imagine used to sit on everyone's desk. It has been particularly beneficial for those in sales, either B2B or B2C, where you may have a high-ticket item and a longer sales journey. In these situations, the value of each contact is higher, and so it warrants more careful collection and use of personal data to sell.

Salesforce has done ridiculously well since its corporation in

1999. According to their website, this is what they do:

'With customer expectations at an all-time high, plus a challenging economy, you need to be as efficient and effective as possible. Salesforce's customer relationship management (CRM) software breaks down the technology silos between departments.

'We call our entire portfolio of products and services Customer 360. It's how you can unite all your teams – marketing, sales, commerce, service, and IT – with a shared view of every customer. Hence, your employees have all the relevant data they need to create incredible customer experiences and grow relationships.'

They have some world-leading tools, but in my experience they are not afraid of relying on heavy selling techniques to push their sales. My own first experience with Salesforce certainly felt forced and a little creepy.

I went to a Salesforce conference in Auckland about four years ago. At the time, companies were starting to realise the growing importance of first-party data, or at least thinking about it as a potential priority in the future.

I remember several times standing and listening to one of the many presentations and starting to feel a little crowded. A couple of times, we were beckoned forward by the speaker and then felt people in the crowd pushing slightly behind me, only to look behind and see some plastered grins pointing past me, directly at the speaker. It felt like they had stooges in the presentations, deliberately pacing forward in unison, nudging people into the talks.

You can customise the sales journey and funnel, but the aim of the game is to move customers through the sales platform. The interconnectivity of the tool means you can do this across departments and have some pretty amazing reporting. It can also be integrated into other Salesforce tools and include programmatic features for scaled communication.

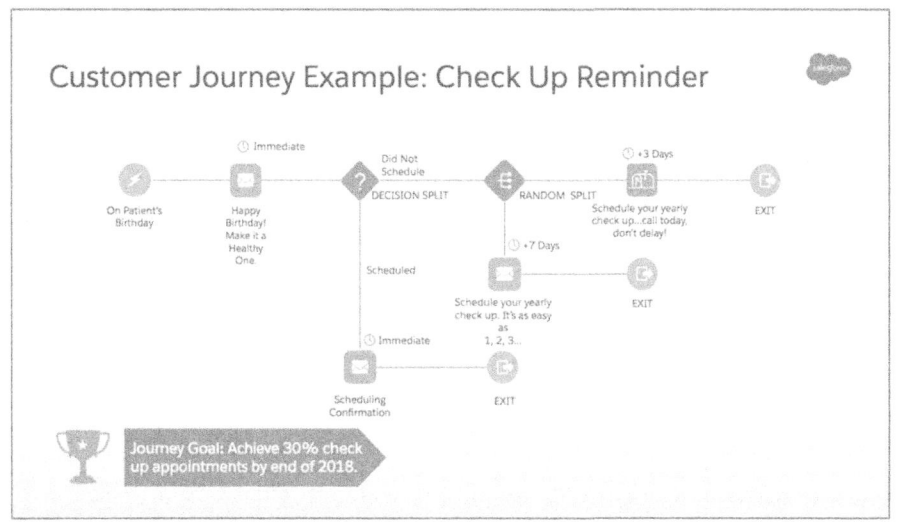

Source: https://www.salesforce.com/

So, what's the problem if it's a great tool? According to Salesforce, 'Customer 360 connects your marketing, sales, commerce, service, and IT teams around every customer so they can work together while boosting productivity, increasing efficiency, and decreasing costs. And with Salesforce Genie, our best-in-class apps are paired with automation, intelligence, and real-time data so you can create customer magic from one trusted platform. That's how you deliver success now.'

Here's the problem: big heavy custom CRM systems and tool stacks tend to be greedy. They don't want to integrate into your MarTech Stack. They want to replace it entirely.

Apart from the growing cost of building a solution like this, your company ultimately becomes entwined with the success of another; the switching cost quite quickly becomes insurmountable.

If your company is considering giving all control to a second company, that's fine. However, it's important to understand the potential risks involved. Allowing a CRM tool to replace all other tools could become problematic in the future, especially if that company increases its costs or falls behind on effectiveness. It's important to carefully consider the long-term implications before making any decisions.

It's worth considering this: What else could we do to reduce or mitigate the risk of becoming overly dependent on one tool? What happens when these companies start cutting back on their R&D and stop supporting certain fringe offerings tools that are no longer profitable?

The main objective is not to dissuade anyone from buying Salesforce or a similar tool. Instead, it's crucial to take a step back and carefully evaluate all relevant factors before making a significant investment.

Based on my experience, large investments in new stacks and tools directly from vendors often fall short of expectations. They tend to exceed the budget because they're oversold, and what the organisation really needed was an honest and unbiased consultation or support to help them make an informed decision.

Before we evaluate whether we need an extensive new CRM tool, we need to take a step back and assess what tools we have now and what might be missing across the whole stack.

8.3 – DATA SOVEREIGNTY

Once seen as only a consideration for a government organisation, data sovereignty must now be a consideration for all. If you use a web analytics tool, where does that data get stored, and who owns it? It's information about your customers and their online experience on your website, but do you actually own that data? If you choose to move tools, can you export it in order to import it into another tool? If your customers ask for their data to be deleted, can you do this easily and cost-effectively?

One of the main reasons why companies switch from free web analytics tools like Google Analytics to paid alternatives like Matomo is the ability to store their data on their own servers within their own country. This is particularly important because there is an increasing concern about the potential risk of sending customer data to offshore data centres in foreign countries without realising it.

Although it's only recently that Google Analytics has been cross-examined due to GDPR legislation in Austria and other European countries, China banned Google Analytics as early as 2015 as part of the Great Chinese Firewall.

What about what tools we choose to use to market to our customers and the data we provide to those vendors in order to target them? Most people are now aware of the Cambridge Analytica scandal. During the 2010s, a British consulting firm named Cambridge Analytica collected personal data belonging to millions of Facebook users without their consent. The primary purpose of this data collection was for political advertising. The data was obtained through an app known as 'This Is Your Digital Life', which was developed in 2013 by data scientist Aleksandr Kogan and his company, Global Science Research.

An app everyone is familiar with is TikTok, but are you aware of who actually owns TikTok? For brands, this could be considered a great place to advertise, but its connections to China are clear. TikTok, also known in China as Douyin, is a short-form video hosting service owned by the Chinese company ByteDance. The owners claim that TikTok is an entirely separate, internationalised version of Douyin. According to Wikipedia, TikTok and Douyin have almost the same user interface but supposedly no access to each other's content. Their servers are each based in the market where the respective app is available.

In May 2021, TikTok's parent company, ByteDance, reportedly ended its contract with Alibaba Cloud and decided to host its servers on Amazon Web Service and Oracle Corporation servers. It isn't clear how much user data is stored on each server or where the company stores its Chinese user data.

At the time of writing this book, both the UK and the USA have started banning government employees from using TikTok company devices. So, it's clear that those governments and their advisers are not convinced by the claim of data sovereignty and separated ownership of data. China, of course, isn't happy about this but is probably not surprised after having initiated their own similar, more far reaching bans as part of the Great Firewall.

Whatever your company decides, there are serious ethical and legal considerations that warrant a close look at every tool in your stack before it's approved, as well as regular review, and if your entire marketing strategy is oriented around TickTok right now, you would surely be getting nervous. As we saw with the

Cambridge Analytica scandal, this is not tinfoil-hat conspiracy thinking any more.

Across the world, governments are seriously worried about the ability of big tech and social media corporations to enable the weaponising of data and the creation of highly targeted advertising for political gain. As ethical marketers, analysts, and consumers ourselves, so should we be.

8.4 – REAL COST

There are a number of unseen costs to review beyond just the tool cost itself, especially if you were to consider a more custom approach.

Some might be opportunity costs of not acting, and some would be actual costs such as subscriptions, consultants, and staff training.

The thing you're looking to build could never happen. In the meantime, the off-the-shelf systems are closer. What's the opportunity cost of not getting started and doing what you do versus constantly discussing, fixing, and customising your solution to enable the doing of what you do?

When a company is attempting a new project for the first time, it's common for the cost to exceed the initial estimate. It's important to keep in mind that many off-the-shelf tools may seem like good value compared to the ongoing expenses of maintaining and operating a custom solution.

The subscription cost of an off-the-shelf tool represents only a small fraction of the total monthly cost incurred by the tool provider to maintain the tool you are using. It's essential to keep in mind that the provider may have hundreds of engineers working on and continuously improving the tool, which may be difficult to replicate in-house.

What are the switching costs of changing solutions if you're looking to invest in a tool? Might you need to rebuild the whole thing again if it doesn't work out?

The actual monthly calculation is usually pretty easy to review, but here is a helpful table. It's worth knowing how costs could increase if your marketing efforts are successful. Most often, vendors will charge by data and/or processing requirements, which could be measured in Users (problematic if Users become duplicated through incorrect tracking), Sessions, or Hits.

Tool	Monthly Cost	Annual Cost	Details
Segment	1200	14500	Business (Connections) - 50,000 Users Per Month (min).
BigQuery	100	1200	Esimated for the first year.
GA4	None	None	Free
Data Studio	None	None	Free
Mixpanel	125	1500	Growth plan - 9,000 User per month.
Hotjar (Heatm;	200	2400	Business - 15,000 Session per month - Two websites.
USD	$1,625.00	$19,600.00	

Source: MckTui Consulting

While revisiting the tool considerations listed above, think carefully about all the possible costs that could surface versus the more predictable costs of an off-the-shelf solution. Is your business case really that special? Just because you *could* build your own custom solution doesn't mean you should. How important are those extra features? How expensive is that monthly fee when taking into account all those other unsurfaced costs? Will the time spent building this thing be valuable and worth it later on when other better options are more widely available in the market?

Big Vs. Small

If you work for a small company, this argument might not seem relevant. The solutions appropriate for a small company differ from those of a large one. A large enterprise may have a much bigger budget and many stakeholders, but a small company has just a few. The problem is that although the bigger company may have a more complex problem to solve, they both have the same underlying issues and barriers to entry. The smaller company just has fewer resources to compete in the same market.

One outcome of the privacy shift is that it directly benefits large companies over small ones. In the past, small companies could access third-party data at a low cost to reach out to potential customers across various publishers and networks without needing to subscribe to additional paid tools or maintain their own audience and first-party data. Google offered free usage of Google Ads and Google Analytics. However, now, companies of all sizes need to build their own audiences instead of accessing others for free. This poses a significant challenge for any company that wants to compete through personalisation. As a result, their advertising becomes less effective and more costly.

It also massively benefits those companies such as Google, Facebook and Apple, who have been slowly amassing huge quantities of consumer data. Where anonymous data was once abundant and freely available, it's now only accessible through these newly created 'Walled Gardens' at a price. Call me a sceptic, but when a big business moves faster than the law in curtailing itself, there is usually a large financial incentive to do so.

8.4 – REAL COST

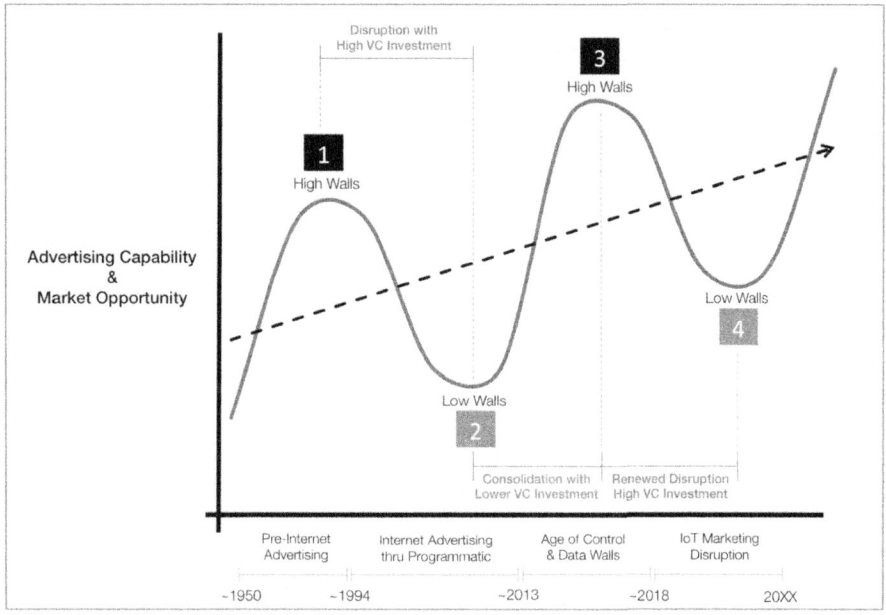

Advertising Capability & Market Opportunity

Chart labels:
- 1: High Walls
- 2: Low Walls
- 3: High Walls
- 4: Low Walls

Top annotations: Disruption with High VC Investment

Bottom annotations: Consolidation with Lower VC Investment | Renewed Disruption High VC Investment

Timeline:
- Pre-Internet Advertising (~1950)
- Internet Advertising thru Programmatic (~1994)
- Age of Control & Data Walls (~2013)
- IoT Marketing Disruption (~2018)
- 20XX

Source: Tom Triscari, CEO at Labmatik.

So, what is a small business to do, and how do they tackle the decisions around purchasing off-the-shelf or custom solutions? The only way forward is to see this decision as a journey and the tools you pack as transferable and only appropriate for different stages. Once you know where we you on the maturity curve, you can set your start and end points and upgrade your team and tools as you go.

It's also helpful to view this problem on a spectrum of small/simple – enterprise/complex. Each company may have its own route but should make decisions as part of a long journey, not based on the pressing issues of the day or a brand-new tool they want to try.

To start, it may be necessary to opt for cost-effective custom solutions that require manual processes. Then, a dual system can be used with separate tools for CRM, email marketing, and web analytics before eventually building a more integrated set of tools. Alternatively, an off-the-shelf tool that is tailored for small businesses or your specific industry could be used in the meantime. The sheer number of options can make this task daunting. Let's work through some of those options.

8.5 – CONSIDERATIONS PER TOOL

As you can see by this hugely detailed image, there are literally thousands of options for tools, but with our variables in place, let's review some of the most popular and those known to have the best modularity.

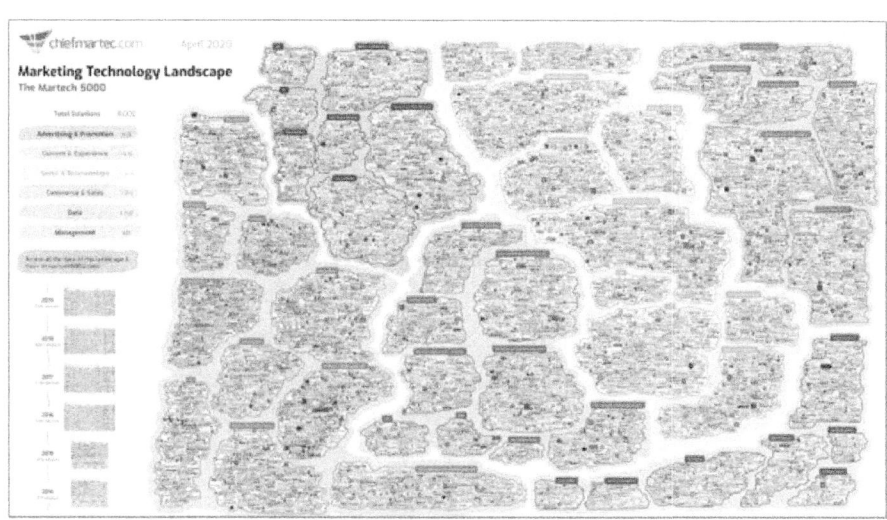

Source: Marketing Technology Landscape; https://chiefmartec.com/wp-content/uploads/2020/04/martech-landscape-2020-martech5000-slide.jpg

Crm (Customer Relationship Management)

With the rise again of first-party data, whatever your service or product, this will always be an essential part of the toolkit. The most popular (or most widely used) are HubSpot, focusing on Content Marketing and Salesforce, centred around B2B sales. As we covered in this chapter, CRM is not THE solution. We need to think broader than just a CRM system and supporting tools from one provider.

Cms/Website

This is another rapidly changing area. One of the first widely used tools was WordPress. Build-it-yourself platforms such as Shopify and Wix are quickly dominating the market. The biggest consideration here is cost vs. control. The cheap version of Shopify is very restrictive regarding what custom tracking can be set up without upgrading to enterprise plans, and enterprise plans are much more expensive.

It's important to carefully examine the capabilities of the website and the shopping cart when considering using affordable solutions. Some cheaper options intentionally limit the customisation options, such as not allowing changes to the shopping cart. It's not necessarily a bad idea to use these affordable solutions, but it's important to be aware that there may be limitations, and the cost may increase in the future. It's best to plan ahead and be prepared for any potential changes.

Database Or Warehouse

Common tools are BigQuery and Snowflake; BigQuery can be suitable for marketers to get started, but for various reasons, Snowflake is a top-rated and affordable solution for most companies and works with cloud database tools like BigQuery.

Snowflake is a cloud data warehouse that can store and analyse all your data records in one place. It can automatically scale compute resources up/down to load, integrate, and analyse data.

This is not to be confused with the equally popular Snowplow. A basic installation of open-source Snowplow collects data really well but does little beyond collecting, cleaning, and saving data in a structured format.

Marketing Automation

HubSpot's free marketing tools make creating a successful marketing campaign that delivers an end-to-end customer experience easy. Create ads, emails, forms, and landing pages all within the same software. There are also paid options and upgrades.

Another popular and often-raved-about tool is Klavyio. They tout themselves as having best-practice e-commerce email experiences to scale repeat purchases right out of the box. Using Klaviyo's AI features, you can segment your audience, generate reports, and forecast performance. Klaviyo also offers automated email flows and dynamic web signup forms.

This should be a destination, not a replacement for web analytics, a CMS, or a key source of information. Like an email platform, it should be a modular output for your marketing campaigns and completely capable of receiving your own custom audiences, not just those created within the platform.

Dashboarding/Reporting

Other than using extensions like Supermetrics, there are popular dashboarding tools such as Looker Studio (formally Data Studio) and paid alternatives at the same level. To drill in-depth into your data and to build self-service dashboards and reports for detailed data analysis in the application, you're normally looking at Microsoft Power BI or Tableau; Microsoft Power BI is often the better value option of the two.

Customer Data Platform

We've already covered a few options here: Segment, Telium, and Acquia. Each has its price points and considerations. Government organisations often use Telium as there is greater control over data sovereignty and where data is hosted and processed. Segment can be more affordable and claims to have more connections.

Web Analytics

It might surprise you, but there are more solutions than Google Analytics; sometimes, a much more suitable solution depending on your requirements.

Matomo, formerly Piwik, is the most common free and open-source web analytics application to track online visits to one or more websites and display reports on these visits for analysis. The open-source element means hosting your own data and avoiding legal issues where your customer data may be passed outside the local region without permission, which is much easier.

Mixpanel and Heap are designed for product analytics where a company provides a SaaS product and wants to understand in detail whether that product is performing. GA4 is more competitive now for this requirement than Universal was.

Adobe Analytics is the only real powerhouse that can compete toe-to-toe with paid GA and the rest of the Google Marketing platform. Adobe Analytics sees itself as part of a more comprehensive end-to-end enterprise-level solution.

GA4 is proving to have more and more development issues, is not currently well supported, and its design is now also more appropriate for web developers and data analysts than marketers. Hence, it may be time to look at alternatives like Matomo for better service (paid) and more stable

◆ ◆ ◆

After reading this chapter, you should feel confident enough to see through the most polished sales pitches and know what crucial questions to ask and the real costs of each approach. You will have some good ideas on what tools to look into and how to review them.

When choosing the right MarTech vendor, clearly define your marketing needs and objectives. Ensure compatibility with your existing technology stack, consider future growth, and prioritise data security and flexibility. Assess the support services and training provided by the vendor. Calculate the total cost, and look for a vendor committed to innovation and know what it means to be over-committed.

Next, we'll look at a key output of all this hard work: we examine the difference between **reports and dashboards**.

We explore whether the elusive Perfect Self-Service Dashboard is a realistic goal worth pursuing and why any two reports rarely add up to the same number.

References And Bibliography

1. Folley, A. (2023). White House announces TikTok ban, legislation amid China tech crackdown. USA Today. Retrieved from https://www.usatoday.com/story/

news/politics/2023/02/28/white-house-tiktok-bans-legislation-what-we-know/11364439002/
2. Hern, A. (2015). Google is returning to China – but should it? The Guardian. Retrieved from https://www.theguardian.com/technology/2015/sep/21/google-is-returning-to-china-it-never-really-lef
3. Rota, Z. (2018). Walled Gardens: Learning from the Past to Predict the Future. AdExchanger. Retrieved from https://www.adexchanger.com/data-driven-thinking/walled-gardens-learning-from-the-past-to-predict-the-future/
4. Chiefmartec. (2020). Marketing Technology Landscape. [Image]. Retrieved from https://chiefmartec.com/wp-content/uploads/2020/04/martech-landscape-2020-martech5000-slide.jpg

CHAPTER 9 – REPORTING VS. DASHBOARDING

In this chapter, we'll look at who needs this data and how, or should we give it to them?

We'll review strategies for collaborating with stakeholders to prevent disappointment and exceed expectations.

We'll try to transform data into tangible wisdom, showcasing the good, the bad, and the ugly aspects of **reporting and dashboards**.

…and review why an apple is not always an apple.

Steady yourself for invaluable insights as we navigate the complexities of data demands and unlock the power of genuine wisdom (not mine, yours).

9.1 – WHO WANTS DATA

Is a dashboard a report, or is a report a dashboard, or are they just the same? Does it matter? This fundamental question drives much confusion around the delivery of data and insights – even around the nature of dashboards: does a dashboard have to be built in a tool like Data Studio and auto-update to be a dashboard, or can it be a collection of graphs and metrics in Google Sheets or static in PowerPoint?

After years of building reports and dashboards for many different stakeholders, I've learnt that it is always best to clear this up before starting anything. Here's my understanding of the issue and the various types of reports and considerations to ensure everyone has the right level of information.

> A dashboard is a visual display of all your must-have data. Think car dashboard. While it can be used in various ways, its primary intention is to provide information at-a-glance, such as KPIs. A dashboard usually sits on its page and receives information from a linked database or API.
> - A report is a specific form of writing organised around concisely identifying and examining issues, events, or findings that have happened in a physical sense, such as events that have occurred within an organisation or findings from research investigation.

So, a dashboard, by definition, is not reporting; it's something you might report on.

The key considerations are to plan and agree on before building a dashboard or writing a report:

- Frequency – how often does the audience need access to the data? And over what period does enough data accumulate for the insights derived to be significant?
- Complexity – how complicated and detailed is suitable for the audience? Do you need all those metrics crammed into one master dashboard?
- Accuracy and Reliability – how important are the accuracy and reliability of the data and the method? This usually links to the importance of the question you're looking to answer and the seniority of the person you're looking to deliver it to or give access to.
- Audience – the most crucial point. Who is this going to be for? The wider marketing team, the CMO or CEO, the head of the department, a colleague, or a customer? How much time and experience do they have to interpret the information you put forward?
- DIKW – Data, Information, Knowledge, or Wisdom. What level of detail and/or formulated conclusions are expected? This can take time and resources and is not always possible. Just because you dig for gold doesn't mean you will find it.

We need to tailor our delivery to each requirement. To do that, we need to ask lots and lots of basic questions and sometimes explain to our audience why what they think they want is not actually what they need. Let's start with the DIKW Pyramid.

9.2 – LEVERAGING THE DIKW PYRAMID

According to Russell Ackoff, a systems theorist and professor of organisational change, the content of the human mind can be classified into five categories:

1. Data: symbols
2. Information: data that is processed to be useful; provides answers to 'who', 'what', 'where', and 'when' questions
3. Knowledge: application of data and information; answers 'how' questions
4. Insights: The appreciation of 'why'
5. Wisdom: Evaluated insights.

Our job is to take our audience through this journey, moving them and ourselves from low-value Data to high-value Wisdom. We can't assume that without our help, our audience can get information, insight, and wisdom from data. We also want to ensure we don't just cherry-pick the data points that prove what they already think is true.

9.2 – LEVERAGING THE DIKW PYRAMID   163

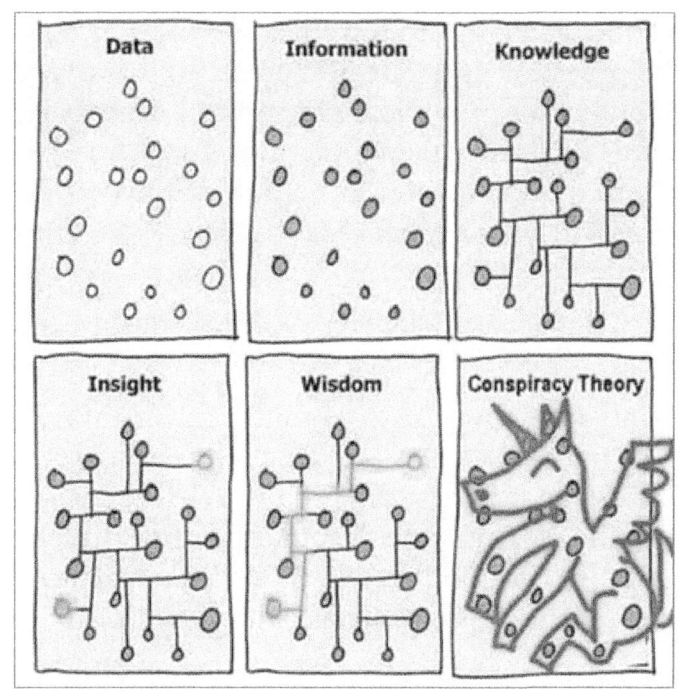

Source: meme adapted from https://www.gapingvoid.com/

Rather than asking whether we need a dashboard or report, the question is, what combination of reporting and dashboards will our business and all our stakeholders need? You need a mix of options for different situations and audiences. Who wants the data and why?

We can then break our considerations into types of 'data presentations':

- Full Access to the data – Data → Information.

This could be Google Analytics or any other data set or platform that collects and displays large amounts of unfiltered and unvalidated data. This is usually what marketing managers and business owners are left with, often causing more trouble and stress than it's worth.

- Self-Service Dashboards (Tactical or Strategic) – Data → Information → Knowledge.

Self-service dashboards for those trained to use them. Open to interpretation, flexible but controlled, with optional dropdowns and filters. Tactical or strategic depending on the audience. Teams should be warned about how often a dashboard's data is checked and reviewed and take any analysis with a pinch of salt. The ability to derive useful information and knowledge will be down to the skill and experience of the user.

- Delivered Dashboards/Reports – Knowledge → Insights → Wisdom.

Delivered at a set time with detailed commentary to a set audience. The data presented in tables or charts will be segmented. Elements presented will be trended over time, and ideally, also indexed against a previously-agreed-upon target for the key performance indicator (KPI). The ultimate goal is to provide timely, useful wisdom for high-value decision-making.

- Commissioned Reports – Knowledge → Insights → Wisdom.

One-off reports that are ad-hoc in nature and might otherwise complicate the existing reporting. These, along with Delivered Dashboards/Reports, should have the highest accuracy.

Those with the right expertise, closest to the data, that understand how it's collected and processed should be trusted with the most access and responsibility for guiding others in the process of extracting actionable business impacts. A big thank you to Avinash for allowing the adaption of this chart – his blog is a must (see source).

Access to Data

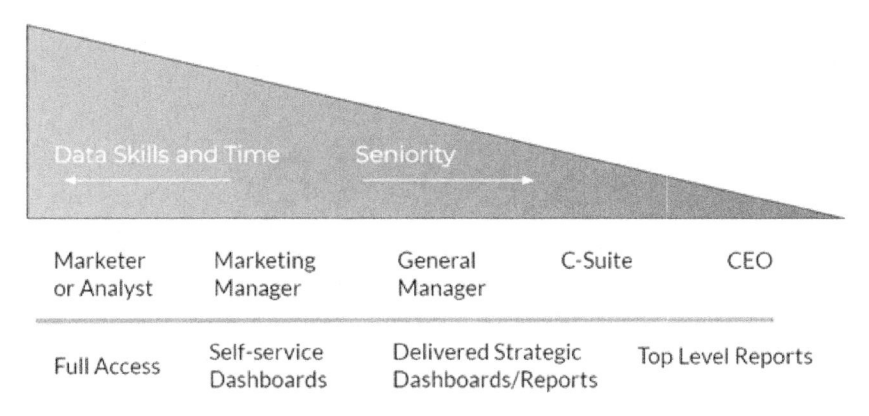

	Marketer or Analyst	Marketing Manager	General Manager	C-Suite	CEO
	Full Access	Self-service Dashboards	Delivered Strategic Dashboards/Reports		Top Level Reports

Source: MckTui Consulting, adapted from https://www.kaushik.net/avinash/digital-dashboards-strategic-tactical-best-practices-tips-examples/

By building all these key variables into a spreadsheet, we can and should build our reporting and dashboard strategic plan before starting. This could form part of our project plan or even live as a separate tab in our measurement plan.

Proposed Reporting Structure - Worksheet

Type of Reporting	Frequency	Complexity	Audience	Accuracy/Reliabilty	Notes
Full Access					
Full Access	Always on	High	Internal and external analytics team	Low	No access given to wider business.
Self-service Dashboards					
Self-service Dashboards	Always on	Medium	Marketing Manager and Product Manager	Medium	Self-service Dashboards for those tr
Delivered Dashboards/Reports					
Strategic Reports	Quarterly	Very Low	CMO,CFO,CEO	Very High	Delivered at a set time with comme
Tactical Reports	Monthly	Low	Department Heads and Managers (non-technical)	High	Delivered at a set time with comme
Commissioned Reports					
CPC Analysis	Ad-hoc	Medium to Low	As required	High	One-off reports that are ad-hoc in n
UX Review	Ad-hoc	Medium to Low	As required	High	One-off reports that are ad-hoc in n

Source: MckTui Consulting.

This lets us clearly define who wants data, why, what, and when – as well as setting and documenting expectations up-front.

9.3 – APPLES TO APPLES

What do we mean by apples to apples in the reporting sense? It means that we ensure we combine two of the same thing, and it's particularly important to ensure this when building reports and dashboards. We have to be certain of what the metrics and dimensions we use actually mean and not just assume what they mean by the name or label they are given. These names represent variables that can change over time, be altered in some way, or even have a similar or the exact same name, but in practice be very different.

Often, your data is not inaccurate. It's accurately telling you something other than what you think it's telling you and leading you or your audience to draw the wrong conclusion.

As we read in Chapter 6 – Plan, Plan, Plan, we need to have our own dimension and metric libraries to ensure that we don't get lost in the actual definitions, and as we saw in Chapter 1 – Climbing the AMC, we need to be sure that data integrity checks and active reconciliation (detailed comparing of like-for-like metrics) are part of our audits. The only sound way to complete a proper data integrity check (apart from regression testing from a previous benchmark) is to compare data sources against each other, and that can often mean comparing MarTech tools and reports like e-commerce reporting to back-end financial systems and accountancy programs that throw up unusual results. It's at this point that we can lose confidence and start worrying that our data might be F**ked.

If we compare the *Sessions* we see in our web analytics tool with the *Visits* reported on our website (often built into the CMS backend), we will see that these are completely different. It doesn't necessarily mean that one of the sources is wrong. They could measure two different, similar-sounding metrics correctly but count them in different ways.

Often 100% accuracy is not possible – in Chapter 4 – Cookie Apocalypse, we explore why, due to the limitations of our tools, we should only expect some metrics to be 95% accurate anyway. The *Revenue* metric we measure in Google Analytics is an example; a 5% variance or less to the revenue recorded in your bank account is more than good enough.

Several reasons can explain an unexpected significant variance in two metrics without their being a problem. Here are some key overlapping factors that can contribute to the mismatch:

1. Data Collection Methods: Differences in data collection methods can lead to discrepancies. If the two sources use different techniques, instruments, or sampling approaches, it can result in variations in the collected data.

As we'll see, Google Analytics 3 collects and then processes data differently from Google Analytics 4.

2. Data Processing Techniques: Variances in data processing methods can also cause discrepancies. Different algorithms, assumptions, or filters applied during data processing can lead to variations in the final results.

This was a key reason why websites used to regularly over-report *Visitors*. Google Analytics had much better access to information about the most recent bots (false traffic created by spammers), which they used to filter out fake sessions automatically.

3. Data Scope and Definition: The scope and definition of the data can significantly impact its interpretation and comparison. The sources' different definitions,

categories, or timeframes for data collection can result in inconsistencies.

A common mistake is comparing *Visits* to *Sessions* or *Users* to *Sessions*. A user has a session on a website and opens a page, which is a *Page View*. These are all different scopes or hierarchies of data.

> 4. Data Updates and Timing: If the two sources were updated at different times, it could lead to disparities. New information, revisions, or corrections made to one source may not be reflected in another, causing discrepancies. Additionally, if the sources have different reporting frequencies or lags, this can further contribute to the mismatch.

This is again different between Google Analytics 3 and Google Analytics 4.

> 5. Data Governance and Standards: Inconsistent data governance practices or varying adherence to data standards can result in differences. It can lead to discrepancies if the sources follow different protocols for data validation, quality control, or normalisation. Additionally, variations in data formats, units of measurement, or encoding standards can contribute to mismatches.

You can control This part of the process by creating and maintaining your own data dictionaries and libraries and sharing them for everyone to review.

We're likely to see this misunderstanding get worse rather than better with the introduction of Google Analytics 4. A GA3 Session is calculated differently from a GA4 Session. They are not the same metric but have the same name, and there are many more examples of these differences. Here are those most likely to cause problems for us marketers.

Key Metrics:

- Sessions: The definition and calculation of sessions can vary between GA4 and G3, leading to differences in session counts.

- Users: The way users are identified and counted can differ between the two versions, resulting in variations in user counts.
- Conversion Rates: GA4 introduces a new way of tracking conversions, which may lead to differences in conversion rates compared to GA3.
- Events: GA4 emphasises event tracking more, allowing more detailed event-based metrics that may not be directly comparable to GA3.

Key Dimensions:

- Traffic Source: The way traffic sources are classified and attributed can differ between GA4 and GA3, leading to variations in traffic source dimensions.
- Device Category: GA4 and GA3 may use different classifications or categorisations for devices, resulting in discrepancies in device category dimensions.
- Content Grouping: GA4 introduces a new way of grouping and organising content, which may lead to differences in content grouping dimensions compared to GA3.
- Campaign Parameters: The handling and interpretation of campaign parameters can differ between the two versions, resulting in variations in campaign dimensions.

Our example here uses Google Analytics as it's such a common tool and just about to go through (depending on when you read this) a huge upheaval.

It is essential to carefully evaluate and understand these factors for each of the different tools that we use, as this is often the only way to identify the root causes of data mismatches and ensure reliable analysis and decision-making. We must ensure we don't mislead naïve users with poor naming, definitions, and labelling, and we can ensure this by both maintaining and auditing our data and libraries.

As we explored in Who Wants Data, we may also need to restrict access to raw data and platforms, ensuring that we only provide guided 'Knowledge and Wisdom' along with the metrics and dimensions we show in our prepared dashboards and reports. This is why we don't leave the analysis to the executives (a key principle suggested in Plan, Plan, Plan). They don't have the time to understand why and how two metrics with the same standard name, from the same tool, with everything working no longer match and why in this previously specialist field that's OK and not completely insane or illogical.

9.4 – THE PERFECT SELF-SERVICE DASHBOARD

Maybe it's down to watching too many sci-fi films, but marketers and analysts often seem to think everything would be good if I had the perfect dashboard. If I give them this collection of tables and bar charts, they will stop asking me stupid questions. I'll finally understand what is happening if I have all the most critical data in one place.

Analytics teams and marketing agencies are most guilty of this; I certainly have been, working at agencies. Dashboarding is comparably cheap and very scalable. We can create a dashboard for on-site metrics, one for SEO, and one for Paid Media, using pre-designed templates, in minutes. Then add some branding and a little design, and you have something that looks custom-designed and professional. Then we can take that dashboard or collection of dashboards and ask an intern to duplicate the process 30–100 times or as many times as we need. Now we're cooking with gas; we've taken care of our contractual agreement to 'report' back to the client in just a couple of hours for all our clients. The clients will look at the dashboards once or twice, perhaps printing some out if there is a disagreement about performance. Still, apart from ensuring the data is available, it's pretty useless and prone to doing more damage than good in the wrong hands.

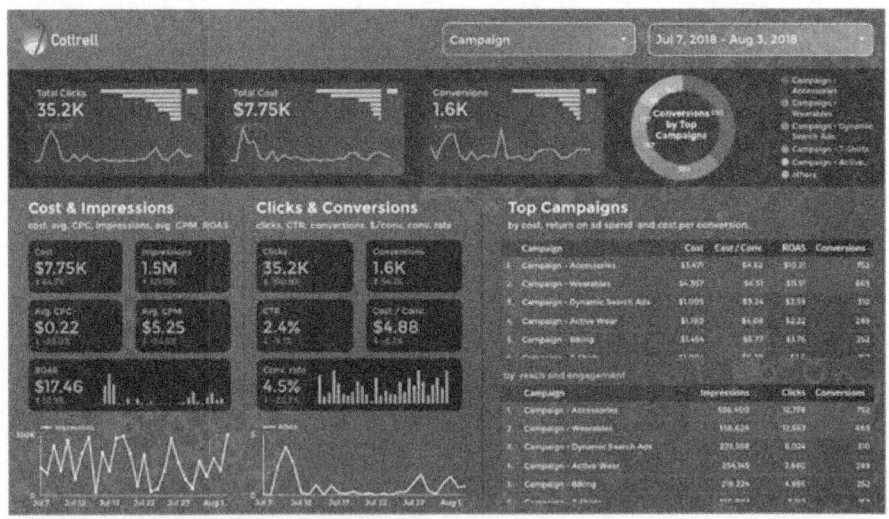

Example Data Studio – Self-Service Dashboard.

Even internal analytics teams do this. They create self-service dashboards for anyone and everyone and expect them to all come to the same interpretation about what is going on with absolutely no context on how the metrics and dimensions are derived or how accurate the data is.

A lot of conversations and mistrust around data is understanding that often two numbers are computed differently and so are not the same. The metric is labelled the same, but you're comparing apples to pears, thinking it's apples to apples.

Finally, let's assume all the data is correct and they understand all the finer details of what you're looking at. It's all written up in Measurement Plans and Libraries, and you should have had a hand in designing your implementations. What about significance? Hundreds of variables could exist between the assumption that A caused B. It can take some time to whittle those variables down to ensure that you look at causation, not correlation or random fluke.

What about human interpretation? I was once asked to review

an e-commerce website's internal reporting; as a successful online retailer, they were flying. They were working hard to progress up the curve, making the most of their existing resources. They had created an exciting weekly report snipping out bits and pieces from various dashboards and circling many impressive-looking metrics and charts. It looked impressive, but it did more harm than good. It gave the impression of continued improvement, which was great until they were not improving. You can make a report that says anything you want by adding or omitting data in different ways.

They had recently changed tack and, in the process, accidentally over-invested in performance ads – by their own judgement. The report showed lovely big jumps in traffic and the desired increased sales, but actually the price for acquiring a new customer was sky-high and unsustainable, so as a consequence, ROI was in the toilet.

For obvious reasons, this kind of reporting, however well-intentioned, can do more damage than good. Without sound interpretation and the right metrics, by missing key context-giving metrics such as cost of acquisition and ROI, they could have continued to invest with a severe case of dashboard blindness. Thankfully the senior leadership knew this and hastily prioritised reviewing their reporting and dashboarding.

When it comes to writing a good report, there are several additional considerations to remember.

Know Your Audience
First, knowing your audience and tailoring the report to their needs is essential. What information do they need to know? How technical should the language be? Answering these questions will help ensure that your report is effective and useful.

Structure
Second, good, predictable organisation is key. A well-organised report is easier to read and understand, so make sure to use

clear headings and subheadings and organise your information logically. This will make it easier for your audience to follow your thought process and understand the information presented.

Talk Like a Human
Third, be concise and avoid using unnecessary words or jargon. It's important to use simple, clear language that is easy to understand, especially if your audience is unfamiliar with the subject matter. Be sure to define any technical terms you use and avoid using too many acronyms or abbreviations.

Be Visual
Fourth, use visuals such as charts, graphs, and tables to help illustrate your points. Visual aids can help make complex information easier to understand and make your report more engaging and interesting to read. Do not expect to have as many visual elements as the dashboard; don't leave any chart or report unexplained.

Check and Check Again
Finally, proofread and edit your report carefully. Spelling and grammar errors can detract from the professionalism of your report, so take the time to review it thoroughly before submitting it to your audience. More so than a dashboard, when providing a report, accuracy is more important, and expect it to take time to progress from Knowledge to Insights and Wisdom.

When it comes to dashboards, the considerations are somewhat different. Dashboards are typically designed for quick and easy access to data and insights, so they need to be visually appealing, be easy to navigate, and provide real-time updates. Information should be presented concisely, clearly, and intuitively, with the most important data highlighted prominently.

Visual design is especially important for dashboards. Use colour, fonts, and other design elements to make the dashboard visually appealing and easy to read. Avoid clutter, and prioritise the most important information. If the dashboard is self-service, use interactive features such as filters and drop-down menus to allow users to customise their experience and focus on the most relevant information.

Writing a good report takes work. It requires careful consideration of your audience, organisation, clarity, use of visuals, and proofreading. On the other hand, designing an effective dashboard requires a focus on visual design, ease of navigation, real-time updates, customisation, and restraint. By thinking about these considerations, you can create reports and dashboards that effectively communicate your message and provide valuable insights to your audience.

Since dashboarding is the most fraught with issues, here are the Ten Commandments I have used myself and with clients when designing dashboards.

1. Buddy System
Metrics need buddies for context. By pairing metrics together, we keep the reader in check and guide their decision-making, preventing dashboard blindness. For example, optimising for clicks or sessions – this is fun and easy. As with our example, the more you spend on your marketing, the more that dial points to success; high fives all around – let's go home. If you place a sanity-inducing metric next to the first, like bounce rate, you get the same information with a little context. Such as, oh crap, we've optimised for clicks, but everyone is bouncing away.

2. Targets and KPI
Each metric should be a key performance indicator. Those KPIs should have pre-agreed targets directly related to the overall marketing or business objective; if you can include those targets on the dashboard next to the KPI, even better. If those key performance metrics have built-in conditional formatting that changes based on whether you are on target or not – great, you're doing analytics in your dressing gown.

3. Tactical or Strategy
Know your audience and use appropriate time frames. If

your dashboard is for the company's CEO, they need top-level information, perhaps five or six key metrics pairs that change colour whether they are on target or not and usually just over the time frame of this month/quarter to the last. They need to see that things are on track.

Suppose your dashboard is for a marketing manager. The information may be plotted over 12 months to map out seasonal trends and campaigns, perhaps breaking the dashboard down by additional dimensions. Don't try and recreate Google Analytics in a dashboard. Look to highlight opportunities or threats focusing on the performance of specific mediums and the website itself.

4. One Page
Keep it to one page and allow the point to be absorbed in five minutes (especially for a strategy-level dashboard). When you drive your car, you don't stare at the dashboard for 20 minutes to grasp its meaning – to tease out your likely speed or speculate whether you need oil. Your car's dashboard is perfectly designed to tell you what you need to know at-a-glance and to alert you to what is wrong and what needs to be investigated now or later.

5. Keep It Visual
Again, keep it visual. Use graphs and conditional formatting. This helps to communicate a lot of information quickly. Like any design, there are dos and don'ts. Don't add unnecessary charts or colours that could distract from what you are trying to show, but use simple graphs in the situations they were designed for.

6. Tell a Story
Like any story, it should follow a framework for beginning, middle, and end. Using a clear framework, you can ensure that the reader follows a simple story every time they read the dashboard. The eggheads at Google provide us with Acquisition (where did they come from?), Behaviour (what did they do?) and Conversions (why do we care?). I prefer to use the old marketing model AIDA – Attention, Interest, Desire, and Action, and

occasionally flip the model so the most important information is at the top.

7. The Right Metric – Funnel
Use the right metrics for the right action in the funnel. Shaping your dashboard around the funnel encourages you to judge your marketing by the appropriate metrics and targets. For example, I've heard positive statements for and against display advertising – the same points of view expressed around above-the-line media such as TV, radio, or billboards for decades. One camp says it's a waste of money; the other says it's not.

It comes down to the sales funnel and ensuring the correct KPIs and expectations for the specific campaign. Display may work fantastically in the top of the funnel, driving awareness for your brand leading to those lizard brain purchases we all make or just creating interest or desire. It may not work well exposed to the harsh light of the action stage, where we are looking at last-click conversions. That doesn't mean it's not worthwhile. If you make more profit with display ads on than switched off, keep using it and keep testing it. Just turning it off because there is no direct ROI, with no plan for testing, is short-sighted.

8. KIS
KEEP IT SIMPLE – so simple that I've simplified this down to KIS. The key reason why dashboards often get out of control is down to vanity metrics and nice-to-know metrics. This is where real restraint is needed, not just to add one more metric.

9. No Vanity or Nice to Have Metrics or Charts.
Avoid nice-to-have metrics that don't relate to KPIs or targets. There are no nice-to-have metrics. No, really, there are no nice-to-have metrics. There is only time and money; you are wasting everybody's time with nice-to-have metrics – especially those metrics that mislead and are only put on the dashboard to make someone look good. This does not mean that we don't track everything necessary. Just don't put everything you can on your dashboard.

10. Know Your Question

What question does your dashboard answer? What is the fundamental purpose of your dashboard? Know ahead of time what answers you plan to ask from it before building and make sure everybody knows what questions it is designed to ask and what story it is telling. If you can't fit in the information for all questions, you may need separate dashboards or reports or to rework your reporting strategy.

If you combine these guiding rules, you will create actionable dashboards in no time and ensure your whole team, whether internal or external, is working towards and kept to task by the same objective.

How can we make sure we don't make these mistakes? On top of ensuring we create reporting for the right person, know that there is no such thing as a self-service dashboard to save all, and if all else fails, check your reporting and dashboarding against the Ten Commandments and considerations – are we trying to crowbar the right requirements into the wrong solution?

A dashboard is a visual display of must-have data that provides information at-a-glance, while a report is a specific form of writing that examines issues, events, or findings that have happened. The key considerations for delivering data and insights are frequency, complexity, accuracy, and reliability, and the audience. Rather than focusing on whether to use a dashboard or report, it is important to determine what combination of reporting the business and stakeholders need. The types of data presentations include full access to data, self-service dashboards (tactical or strategic), delivered dashboards/reports, and commissioned reports.

Marketers and analysts often set out to create the perfect self-service dashboard. More often than not, that's the problem. One dashboard is not enough for everyone and under all circumstances. We need to tailor our delivery to each requirement. To do that, we need to ask lots and lots of basic questions and sometimes explain to our audience why what they think they want is not actually what they need.

This process can be uncomfortable and requires good personal skills; building the dashboard is the fun part, which is why the requirement-setting and strategy part is so often missed. But the more information you have to understand your audience's needs, and the more you can lead your stakeholders in addressing the wider strategy of reporting and dashboarding, the better results you will have and the better chance you will have to deliver and land real, lasting business value.

◆ ◆ ◆

We're riding high on top of the DIKW Pyramid, dispelling the myth of the perfect all-use, self-service dashboard. We've collected some guiding rules and principles for building a **great dashboard and writing an actionable report**.

Up next, we need help to do this – we explore the essential skills, knowledge, and abilities required to bridge the gaps.

We'll dive into the decision-making process of bringing in external expertise or outsourcing certain tasks and **how to organise and serve our team better by using Tracks**.

References And Bibliography

1. Kaushik, A. (2012). Digital Dashboards: Strategic & Tactical: Best Practices, Tips, Examples. [Blog post]. Occam's Razor. https://www.kaushik.net/avinash/digital-dashboards-strategic-tactical-best-practices-tips-examples/
2. Kaushik, A. (2006). Five Rules for High-Impact Web Analytics Dashboards. [Blog post]. Occam's Razor. https://www.kaushik.net/avinash/five-rules-for-high-impact-web-analytics-dashboards/

3. Portent. (n.d.). One Trick to Set Strategic Goals Your Business Needs: Focus. [Blog post]. Portent. https://www.portent.com/onetrick/#setstrategicgoals
4. Klipfolio. (2018). 10 Tips for Better Dashboards. [Blog post]. Klipfolio. https://www.klipfolio.com/blog/10-tips-for-better-dashboards
5. Ackoff, R. L. (1989). From Data to Wisdom, Journal of Applied Systems Analysis, Volume 16, 1989 p 3–9.

CHAPTER 10 – WHO IS MISSING?

This chapter outlines the crucial aspect of defining roles and responsibilities. We create distinct career paths for individuals with both soft and hard skills, acknowledging the value they bring to the table. We break down the required skills into two key tracks of specialisation, and provide clear examples of the work involved in each track.

Furthermore, we address the **structural divides, both internal and external, that contribute to siloed work environments and perpetual institutional amnesia**. Our exploration aims to identify solutions that foster collaboration, break down barriers, and promote knowledge sharing.

We navigate the realm of roles, specialisations, and collaboration, seeking to build a cohesive and productive environment that maximises the potential of every team member.

10.1 – WHO DOES WHAT?

That's all well and good, but who will do this work? Should I hire, learn the skills myself, or look to bring in an external company? As always, it depends, but let's work through some key determining factors, what the work is, and how it is typically divided, as well as the problems that can come from this division.

If you pull this off, you'll need a team, in-house or external; it's good to know what types of roles you will need and how they may connect to your existing team and capabilities. Eventually, your organisation should plan to own, understand, and manage your tracking and data, building the wisdom required to enable impactful analysis.

It's helpful to get an idea of the typical roles and the knowledge, skills, and abilities they should have. I've built teams that supported clients as external providers and integrated so closely that the external team acted as the client's internal analytics team. I've also built teams from within a company as part of an acquisition. I saw first-hand the difficulties that companies face in integrating analytics into their everyday work.

F**ked data can often be down to a skills shortage. Often it's structural, company-wide undervaluing of the work and the people that do data and analytics. An organisation may need to champion and empower the person or people holding the keys to good data.

So how do we pick or build our A-team, and who are the key players? This task is more formidable to those jacks of all trades in smaller companies, as if you don't have the budget, you will need to assign these additional roles through your current team and reduce the scope or timeline of what you're looking to achieve.

Roles –
Existing Team Executive

- Executive Sponsor – this person is responsible for the project or department without being in the analytics department and reports to the rest of the senior leadership team. They advocate for better data generally. They understand the overall Business Strategy and goals. This could be a CMO, CEO, director, or another member of the C-suite.

- General or Performance Marketer – probably you: you're fed up of having F**ked data, and hopefully, you have some backing from an Executive Sponsor to get it sorted. Your skills are not in Web Analytics, but you're ready to give it a go or have had it shoe-horned into your current responsibilities, Mr or Ms Jack-of-all-trades. You understand the Marketing Strategy and how it relates to the Business Strategy.

- Product Owner – sometimes wrapped into the above, but they are often responsible for the User Experience on the website for all products or one product, depending on the company size. Weirdly enough, they can often be part of the problem if, coming from more of a design background, they may prefer to either find the numbers that support what they already think or run on gut instincts. They are often a gatekeeper to accessing the developers and ensuring tracking is regularly maintained.

Existing Team Enablers

- Business Analyst – having a good BA is often gold. They can assist in writing the measurement plan, developer instructions, and project plan by working with the analytics team and Executive.
- Project Manager – a Project Manager can ensure everyone stays to scope, timeline, and budget. They are essential to larger projects with many tools, brands, and web assets.
- Web Developer – most tracking will require some level of implementation. Sometimes the developer will be in-house, and sometimes they will be part of a web development company. Their key role is to add the code as requested, where requested, ensure it does not conflict with the regular running of the website or app, and be there to troubleshoot if something is not working.

Core Analytics Team
- Web Analytics Specialist – an essential person to the project's success. They will help create the developer instructions, check their implementation, and be there to troubleshoot with the web developer if something is not working. They may have been a web developer or designer at some point but have since seen the error of their ways and come to the light.

- Data Analyst and Reporting – they work with the Marketers to understand what to track. They may have the support of the BA if you're lucky. They will support the team in what reporting or dashboards will be built later. Their area of focus is to provide support in utilising data effectively to benefit executives and other stakeholders. This includes providing insights and analysis to aid decision-making and improve overall performance.

- Strategist, Head of Analytics or Growth (new buzz

term) – depending on the difficulty of the project, this role may or may not be needed. This could also be you after reading this book because if no one else is going to do it, you might as well do it yourself. They lead the analytics team and act as the vital connection between the enablers, the analytics team, and the Executive. They understand the goals of all and recommend what should be done, OR perhaps they are the core analytics person on the team and are also expected to be a jack-of-all-trades.

GAP Analytics Team

They're all nice to have, really nice to have, but often only required in larger implementations. Their roles are absolutely essential in moving from levels 1–3 to 4–5, and not having these skills is part of 'The GAP' – another way small companies find it difficult to progress without being locked into one system.

- Data Engineer –can help make the Solutions Architect design work connect up. Lives for data pipelines and conversations about ETL and creating databases.
- Data Scientist –here to create fantastic data models, prove significance, predict, clean, and work with big data sets.
- Solutions Architect – The visionary, the draftsman, the designer of the house we'll all work in.

Where do you fit in? Maybe you don't. Look at this list and see what roles could be missing and may need to be assigned.

10.2 – THE TWO TRACKS

I was often asked to give talks to various universities about what I look for when building a team. Unless you are a consultant, you fall into one of two camps. The more technically focused with 'hard skills' or people-focused with 'soft skills'. I refer to these as Track One and Track Two.

Just like with our tools, where possible, we should look to specialise, if only to keep up. There are many analytics consultants out there; I should know – I was one of them, but the goal of building a team should not be to develop more consultants or replace your existing consultant with one in-house. We should look to build excellence; to do that, we need to focus and specialise.

One of the key differences between the two tracks is soft and hard skills. Soft skills are personal attributes that enable someone to interact effectively and harmoniously with other people. Hard skills are objective, quantifiable skills gained through training, school, or work experiences. Hard skills are often something that can be taught or learnt. For that reason, hard skills can typically be easily proven — you either know how to write code or you don't.

One of the mistakes companies make is rewarding soft skills over hard ones. Of course, we're all people, and soft skills are essential for general harmony, but the level required only matches the role and the task. If you're an excellent coder, why should you also need to manage clients or suppliers? By creating two tracks, we can value both types of skills and maintain some degree of order.

Many great web analytics specialists may believe that to advance in their careers, they must either manage other analytics specialists or transition into a managerial role that demands a high level of soft skills. Instead of this, they could choose to deepen their expertise in analytics, specialise in a specific area, or broaden their knowledge across various tools and technologies, such as building their proficiency in the MarTech stack.

	Track 1 – Hard Skills
Track 1	Data Development
Traditional Roles	Data Scientists, Data Engineering, Web Development (data), Solution Architecture
KPIs	Data Accuracy, Completed Hours

	Track 2 – Soft Skills and Business-Informed Analysis
Track 2	Analysts and Strategists
Traditional Roles	Project Managers, Data Analysts, Business Analysts, Strategy and Consulting
KPIs	NPS Score, Managed Hours, Team Growth

We can take those roles and break out a path to development depending on what the team member is interested in. For example, Track 1 could be something like this:

Possible Roles, Skills, And Knowledge For Track 1

Digital Solutions

Solution design
Self-Service dashboard and report building
Analytics library design
Data engineering
Data science
Broad MarTech tool knowledge
Technical lead

Role 1 – Digital Solutions Architect
Python – Core coding skills
SQL – Core coding skills
Big Query – Platform knowledge
Microsoft Power BI – Platform knowledge
Segment – Platform knowledge

Role 2 – Analytics Development Specialist
Analytics Registry – Design and creation
MarTech Tool – In-platform configuration
Developer instructions and support
JavaScript – Core coding skills
Measurement Events and dataLayer – Design and creation

Here the skills required mean the person and work are closer to the code and hands-on development. With enough deep knowledge of more than one tool and an expanded understanding of how tools could integrate, a role could naturally progress into a Senior Analytics Development Specialist or, with further training, a Solutions Architect.

Possible Roles, Skills, And Knowledge For Track 2

Strategist and Data Insight

Workshopping
Personalisation and data strategy
Measurement planning
Training facilitator
Reporting strategy and design
Actionable insights
Stakeholder management

Role 1 – Senior Strategist and Data Insight

Tealium – In-tool use and strategy
GTM – In-tool use and strategy
Data Studio – In-tool use and strategy
Mixpanel – In-tool use and strategy

Role 2 – Reporting and Data Insight Specialist

Basic measurement planning
Insights and reporting
Tool configuration (no code)
Basic training
Customer service

Once the tools are set up, a Reporting and Data Specialist would work more closely with key stakeholders to get the data; they are sometimes required to configure tools themselves and build dashboards and reports. The distinction between different the tracks in web analytics may depend on whether the task requires coding or not. Some professionals may choose to specialise in specific tools or a group of tools and have a deep understanding of the strategic importance of using these tools in achieving business goals.

Where Track 1 is closest to coding and creating the solution, Track 2 is closest to the stakeholder and understanding the many facets of the problem; some of these could be entirely human and political in nature. Neither is more important than the other, and both are sides of the same coin.

10.3 – THE DIVIDE

Great, we have a good idea of who should be on the various teams and tracks and what everyone should be doing. We can formally break this across a RACI chart (Responsible, Accountable, Consulted, Informed) and include it in our Project Plan. We can also decide when and how these teams should meet in our Communication Plan, how the analytics function should be structured within the company, and when various stakeholders should be consulted. Most importantly, we can assign proper accountability.

Let's go back to our Marketing Stack. Analytics sits firmly at the foundation of any marketing campaign or website change. It's second only to properly maintaining our infrastructure. Another reason our data is often F**ked is that we don't maintain it, which is why accountability and responsibility are essential. If we continually make changes to our website and apps without building analytics as a recurring task, we will continue to break it.

Product Development Cycle

A Product development cycle should be like a CRO cycle:

Continuous Improvement

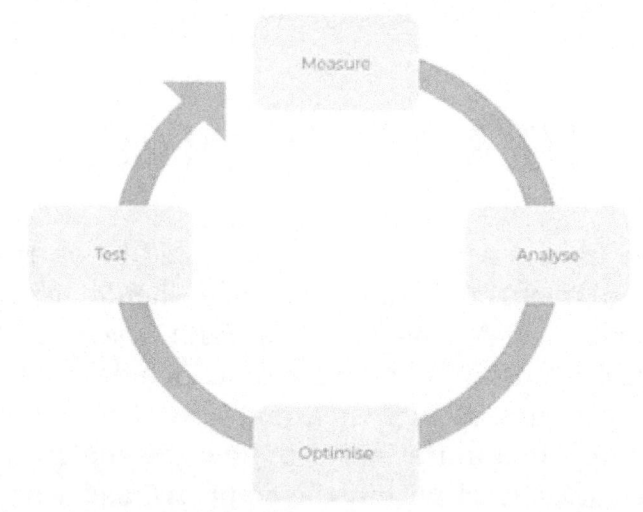

Source McKtui Consulting, based on Eisenberg, B., & Eisenberg, J. (2005). Call to Action: Secret Formulas to Improve Online Results. Thomas Nelson.

Often, it's not because there are so many things people want to improve or fix. CRO often fails to deliver or show clear returns on investment because bad UX is death by a thousand cuts rather than some big profitable change that can be identified to fix everything. Actual continuous improvement requires continuous measurement, analysis, optimising, and testing. And faith.

To understand your data and move to impactful insight and, finally, wisdom, those accountable for tracking must know you're making changes to the website or app. They need to be informed or consulted, and measurement plans must be updated. If you want them to support you in analysis and understanding whether your improvements were actual improvements, then the analyst also needs to have been part of the discussion, implementation, and results to have enough information to sift through the data. They need some knowledge of what has transpired and why, to give you an understanding of whether it worked.

Constantly working through a wishlist of changes from multiple points of view and stakeholders is like forever chasing your tail, and when you succeed, how confident can you be that it was down to your actions and not just a fluke catch? This is where a smaller organisation can have more success. There are fewer teams, fewer variables, and fewer other things happening. They're often closer to the problem and the possibility of a sound judgement based on gut feeling, but with a corporation and big brands, just proving causation can be impossible, and a sounder method is needed.

Whether they are internal or external, bring your analytics team out of the cold and keep them up to date. Avoid kneejerk actions and reactions, and be methodical. A lucky win now is not worth the sustainable small gains from genuine, reliable continuous improvement. If you do this, you can't lose because every loss will contribute to the overall learning and win. This is a true cause to be championed and supported.

I worked with a company that, for a period, worked hard to understand its sales funnel. They implemented detailed Tier 3 tracking for every field, maintained that tracking, and included analysts in their product discussions. Over time, conversion rates increased, and hundreds of thousands of dollars were plugged in their once-leaky funnel. Then leadership changed, and the teams became complacent. They stopped adding unique ID elements to their fields for easy tracking, updating measurement plans, and maintaining their field tracking reports. They moved to a new tool that promised automated tracking.

It didn't deliver as expected. All that happened was that instead of labelling unique identities for fields in their dataLayer, they had to start configuring the same identification in the tool retrospectively. None of that data or work could be shared in other tools, and they steadily became locked in. The new tool got snowballed, and they began moving to a 3rd tool without any of the updated measurement plans to support them and with the additional tasks of auditing and reworking all the patchy and now incomplete tracking. To say that it was expensive learning is an understatement.

Specialisation Without Silos

Let's go back to our Marketing Stack. Analytics sits firmly at the foundation of any marketing campaign or web development change.

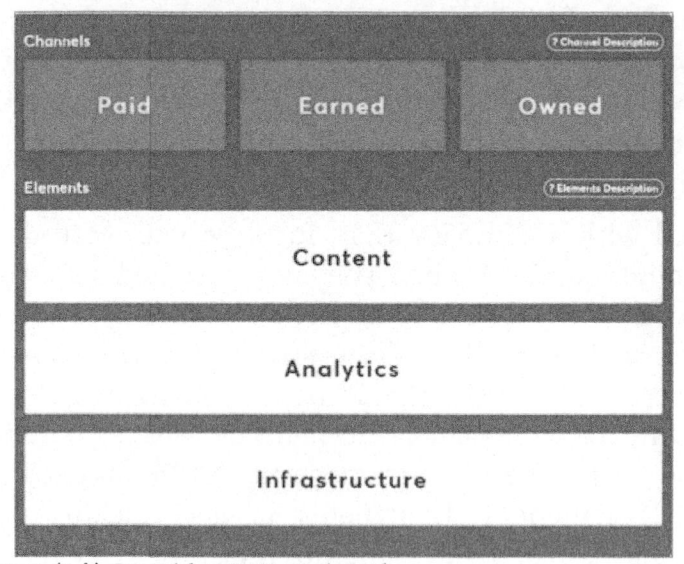

```
Channels                                      (? Channel Description)
    Paid            Earned           Owned

Elements                                      (? Elements Description)
              Content
              Analytics
              Infrastructure
```

Source: Portent. (n.d.). One Trick to Set Strategic Goals

To stop circling and moving back up and down the Analytics Maturity Curve. We need to both encourage competitive specialisation and simultaneously remove siloed thinking. So, how can we do that? What's the best compromise?

A marketing agency or internal department can be siloed in many ways: sometimes the department itself from other departments, but often as per our stack, it's by channel or element. One of the ways we can allow for specialisation and still avoid siloed thinking is to ensure matrix teams as part of our projects.

Matrix teams are cross-functional teams that bring together individuals from different departments or areas of expertise to work on a specific project or task. They allow for collaboration and knowledge sharing while avoiding siloed thinking.

We can also create roles that focus on what we want the output to be, such as Head of Personalisation and the traditional CMO, but also define the difference between departments. This does go some way to explain some of the more lofty-sounding titles.

Analytics and Infrastructure (as per the Marketing Stack), or your web developer, depending on the company and team, are not just a department. They need touch on everything, so they are core enablers for other functions. Let's look at how most digital agencies are organised.

Agencies offer services to Marketers; some agencies offer jack-of-all-trades consultants with varying competency levels. However, most focus and specialise in paid, social, content, or SEO. The agency may have a web development business, but usually, that's an entirely different company. If you are a small company, it's external. If you're large, it's an internal department, often run very differently from the marketing team. Then we have the Project Managers, Account Managers, and Salespeople. On top of that, some form of leadership. Analytics often comes out of either web or paid. Paid because that's why Google bought Urchin to prove the value of AdWords through Google Analytics and Web because they're given the job of putting stuff on the website.

How To Avoid The Divide

The Divide

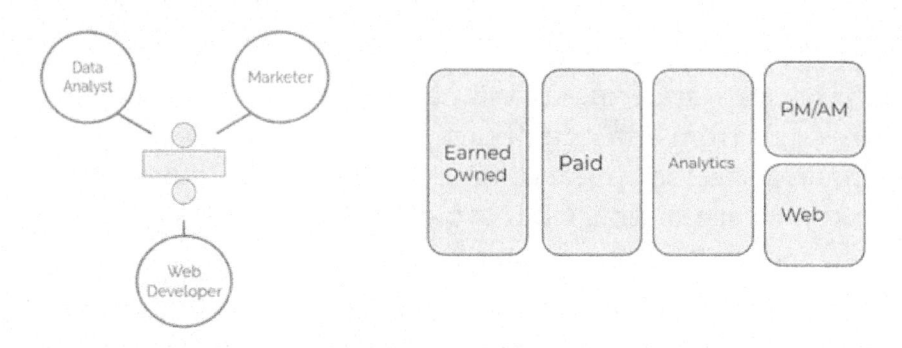

Source: Mcktui Consulting. Traditional Divides.

This structure creates a common divide between Web developers and Marketers. For example, to set up web analytics correctly, Marketers need help on how best to structure the data being collected by the tool, especially with the new GA4. How do we effectively transition from Event, Label, and Action to value pairs or parameters and variables? The Data Analyst will probably need help from the Web Developer to add the correct tracking. Often this work will need to be completed on a one-off basis with very little documentation or governance or additional support in a siloed structure. Our example shows Earned and Owned, like Content and SEO, sitting separately from Paid and Analytics, with Web and management functions separated again (Project Managers, Managers, or Account Managers).

10.3 – THE DIVIDE

[Diagram: Three columns labeled "Earned Owned", "Paid", "PM/AM" sitting on top of stacked foundation layers: "Documentation and Governance", "Analytics", and "I.T, Infrastructure and Web Development". A circular arrow loops around the PM/AM column.]

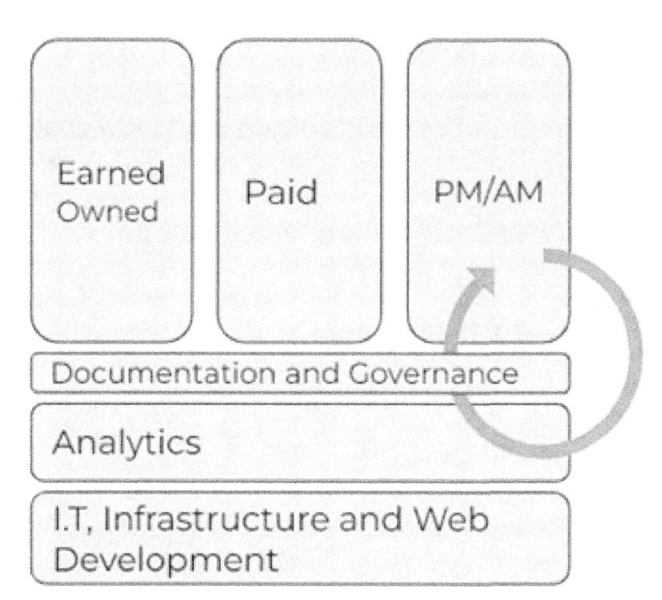

Source: Mcktui Consulting – Suggested Structure.

A much better way to organise our stack is to ensure our most critical departments are structured as foundations touching all other departments, rather than as additional silos. In our Suggested Structure, we have Analytics supporting Channels alongside IT infrastructure and Web Development, with a necessary support barrier of Documentation and Governance.

This would include changes to the websites or apps and content. At the same time, they are a unifier across channels and supporting real omni-channel marketing and personalisation. They can collect good data, give information, build knowledge and wisdom, and offer a real impact. The organisation as a whole can be infused with data-led decision-making and avoid the serious disruption of infrastructure and tracking breaks.

Of course, to do this, we need to stop chasing our tails and sacrificing short-term wins for long-term gains.

◆ ◆ ◆

Excellent, now you know who you need and how best to organise them.

You know that F**Ked data isn't all your fault (unless it is), and you walked into a situation that was already poorly organised before you got there, but can and should work differently.

Next up:

PART THREE – **WHERE DO WE GO FROM HERE?**

References And Bibliography

1. Eisenberg, B., & Eisenberg, J. (2005). Call to Action: Secret Formulas to Improve Online Results. Thomas Nelson.
2. Portent. (n.d.). One Trick to Set Strategic Goals Your Business Needs: Focus. [Blog post]. Retrieved from https://www.portent.com/onetrick/
3. Hayajneh, H., Herrera, M., & Zhang, X. (2021). Design of combined stationary and mobile battery energy storage systems. PLoS One, 16(12), e0260547.
4. What Are Hard Skills? Definition and Examples - Forage. https://www.theforage.com/blog/basics/hard-skills

PART THREE – WHERE DO WE GO FROM HERE?

What a journey! If you have come this far, thank you for reading. The good news is that you are 80% through and ready to roll up your sleeves and start unF**king your data and pushing for real, sustainable digital transformation and growth through one-to-one ethical personalisation strategies. You also know that the last sentence wasn't wholly made-up. But I could have, and we should work hard to explain what we do in an accessible and simple way.

More on this in our conclusion.

In this next section, I'll make **five critical predictions** for the big things we will see happening months or even years from now. Who will be the **Winners and Losers** of all this change, what part will AI play, and why do I think those people working in roles more aligned to **Track 2 jobs are safer**, at least for now?

I'll talk about how and why I think we'll now start seeing real change in our daily lives and where to look for great personalisation as a customer. Whatever happens, the sometimes opposing macro-forces of social change and technological change will continue to play out in the courtrooms, meaning much **more money to lawyers** and those filing suit. Also, I'll suggest how and why the recent **tech wreck** and massive downsizing of tech employees for nearly all the major social platforms and SaaS platforms will directly impact our own MarTech Stacks and marketing plans.

Then, I'll summarise what we've worked through and why marketers continue to have F**ked data, and why a **lack of investment and understanding** continues to be one of the biggest drivers of this. I'll examine how offering Google Analytics for free could have contributed to the **lack of perceived value of analytics**, and what could be next for Google and the big tech platforms that build the roads we all work and play on.

Finally, we'll hug, cry, and I'll send you on your way with some parting advice from a well-known and eccentric genius.

CHAPTER 11 – TIMES ARE A-CHANGIN'

In this chapter, we'll first look back, pausing to contemplate the present before setting our sights on the future.

We will explore **five critical predictions** that anticipate significant shifts, some of which may unfold in the coming months or even years.

But it's not all sunshine and rainbows. We also confront serious concerns that impact both marketers and customers alike. We navigate the exciting landscape of the future, exploring possibilities, challenges, and the ever-evolving dynamics that shape our industry.

11.1 – PREDICTIONS AND REFLECTIONS

Will our data always be F**ked? What could f**k our data in the future? It's time for us to make our own predictions of the future – the big things we see happening months or even years from now.

George Santayana, an American philosopher, said: 'To know your future, you must know your past.' While researching this book, I came across an article making future predictions. John D. Louth, a writer for the McKinsey Quarterly, spoke about 'the changing face of marketing' as far back as 1 September 1966; he wrote:

'Change is the dominant fact of life in every business today. And the ability to master and exploit change has become one of the most sought-after management skills. This is particularly true in marketing, where the very tempo of change is constantly quickening.

'The dominance of the customer

'It is nearly a truism that the needs and wants of the consumer are the critical issues today in creating new products and services and developing the accompanying plans to merchandise them at a profit. But this trend – the first on my list – is still in the process of evolution. The need to understand and anticipate future customers is bound to become even more essential than in the past, because the end users of almost every company's products are shifting in makeup, location, and number at an ever-increasing rate.

'The significance of this to senior marketing executives is twofold: First, they cannot – indeed, they must not – assume that yesterday's customers will be available tomorrow. Second, they had better be certain that they have adequate sources of market information. Unless they can keep up with what is happening to their markets, the whole company's selling effort may ultimately be directed at the wrong people with the wrong products and at the wrong time. This is what a marketing vice president I know meant when he said, "My company's sales output can't be any better than my intelligence input."'

Perhaps our methods might change with the technological and social landscape around us, but what we're trying to achieve in the changing landscape does not. Just like our market trader example, modern data and analytics are just about trying to achieve personalisation at scale – offering the right products to the right people at the right time. Sixty years ago or 60 years from now. It always comes back to how well you know and serve your existing and prospective customers.

I predict the following five things driven by political, economic, social, and legal factors that will drive the next five years in digital analytics for marketing.

11.2 – PREDICTION 1 – WINNERS AND LOSERS

The winners and losers of all this change will not be who you think or even who was intended to benefit from them.

Facebook, Google, and other large tech publishers of information will continue squeezing agencies out of the market by developing AI, leveraging data, and improving their direct-to-market capabilities of ad-purchasing tools.

The ultimate victors of further legislating and restricting the storage, movement, and use of customer data will be larger companies and owners of the aforementioned 'walled gardens', now ready for harvesting: the companies collecting information for decades and providing purportedly free services to use their platforms. Not the consumer and not the businesses paying for advertising to service their customers. Until some form of technology can give direct consumers ownership over their data to sell as needed, big tech platforms will win more from this change than consumers.

Small and big businesses will be forced to pay more to activate their customer data. They will need to do this directly through big platforms, paying more for the privilege, improving their own marketing stacks, and increasing their capability. The companies providing this technology, typically SaaS companies and big tech, will profit in this increasingly competitive environment.

'Ongoing data privacy disruptions and consumers' accelerated adoption of digital channels are upending traditional ad placements. Digital marketing leaders should prepare by exploring how leading brands adapt ad efforts within the walled gardens of YouTube, Amazon, and Facebook.'

-Gartner

Nearly four out of five US digital advertising dollars are spent with walled garden publishers like Google, Meta, Amazon, and Apple. Legislation put in place to protect consumers and shift the balance of power will do this successfully, although occasionally rapping the knuckles of those testing the new legislation. Ultimately these companies stand the most to gain.

It's not all doom and gloom, as it's hoped that after more data and wider opportunities become available through smart technology and the Internet of Things, we will begin to see greater marketing opportunities open up again.

11.3 – PREDICTION 2 – TRACK 2 HAS MORE DISTANCE

Track 2 (Analysts and Strategists) will be safer than Track One (Data Development), at least initially, from increasing AI and tool sophistication.

Where Track 1 is closest to code and creating the solution, Track 2 is close to the stakeholder and understanding the many facets of the problem. These problems are more likely to be more human and political in nature and so less predictable or patternable.

On writing this, the news was awash with ChatGPT, along with the image generators like Midjourney or Crayon AI that can be used to create weird trippy art and pictures. If you need a picture of a pizza in a dishwasher, this is now possible at the touch of a button, with plausible detail. Of course, the application of Crayon AI is much broader. An AI model that can draw images from any text prompt has the potential to revolutionise various industries, from design to education, by automating the creation of visual content in a fast and cost-effective way.

11.3 – PREDICTION 2 – TRACK 2 HAS MORE DISTANCE 207

Source: https://www.craiyon.com/

ChatGPT has obvious immediate opportunities for already formulaic writing used prevalently in digital marketing, such as writing performance ad copy and content for design to appeal to search engines rather than people, but don't take my word for it. The following was prompted by me but written and unedited by ChatGPT:

'The rise of AI is affecting the job market and making some roles vulnerable to automation. AI is being used in various industries, from manufacturing to healthcare. As AI evolves and becomes more sophisticated, the types of jobs that are most at risk of being replaced by AI will change. Administrative roles are highly vulnerable to automation, including data entry and customer service tasks. Customer service jobs can be replaced by AI-powered chatbots that can respond quickly and accurately to customer queries. Transportation roles are also at risk as autonomous vehicles are becoming increasingly common. Finally, roles in banking and finance can be automated with AI algorithms that can automate financial processes and provide financial advice. While the short-term impact of job loss is concerning, the long-term future could also bring new opportunities. It is crucial to note that AI cannot replace human creativity, and there will still be a need for human involvement in many areas.'

The applications are truly staggering at this stage, although prompting and validation are still needed. We need people to create prompts for the AI and work on revisions back and forth, whereas the heavy lifting is automated and reformulated based on online information already available; the actual seed of creation and validation is still coming from us.

However, AI is already moving so fast that it's hard to know how far this will go. At the time of writing this book, the 'godfather' of AI had just disowned his own creations: 'The man often touted as the godfather of AI has quit Google, citing concerns over the flood of misinformation, the possibility for AI to upend the job market, and the "existential risk" posed by the creation of a true digital intelligence.' – The Guardian.

The limitation of automated intelligence, which could be very good for us as a species, is that it does not understand what it's doing. There is no self. A good example of this is the comparison between Go and Chess. AI is excellent at Chess, but it can't play Go, at least well enough to beat most good human players. The reason is that Go typically has too many variables to compute, and the machine learning programs also find it very difficult to anticipate humans deliberating trying to trick them. They are just following the pattern-like structure of any code; if they do this, then I should do that. They don't know they are playing Go against a human or anything else.

This is why soft skills like people skills within Track 2 will have more distance than those in more programmatic skills in Track 1. AI is here to make humans more efficient and effective; it won't replace humans, at least not yet, but marketers using AI will replace marketers not using AI.

11.4 – PREDICTION 3 – ANTICIPATION BECOMES REAL

As more businesses move from prescriptive analytics to predictive analytics, we will start seeing real-world uses of this technology affecting our daily lives; benefits like this will encourage more customers to share more data as the benefits become more natural.

A few years ago, the tech space was awash with in-home AI assistants. It felt like we would start to see the smart home come to life with the use of Google Home or Amazon's Alexa. Like most, I dabbled briefly but immediately became concerned about having a microphone in my house and realised this was still new unregulated technology. I didn't know where the data was stored and for how long, so I put my device away. How many of my personal, albeit mostly dull and humdrum, conversations would end up on a server somewhere? These were my concerns as a consumer, and then a little later, I started listening to talks on the application and potential of performance search for the voice and future applications for clients.

Lots of people I knew started using them to play music. 'Hey, Alexa, play lounge jazz', but nothing more out of all the potential applications seemed practical. Then we started hearing the inevitable stories of strange incidents with random products arriving in the post and whole conversations being packaged

11.4 – PREDICTION 3 – ANTICIPATION BECOMES REAL

up and sent to random friends and family. Although these incidents were few and far between, it was certainly enough to make people start thinking about these listening devices' costs and potential risks. Without more real-world applications, is it worth having a voice-activated, possibly temperamental listening device in the house?

'…however, data-steered innovations have threatened security and privacy, creating hindrances for the global smart speaker market. The market was worth US$ 10.34 Billion in 2022.

'Sales continue to grow, as do the applications of the new technology increase with safeguards for data and rogue AI's.'

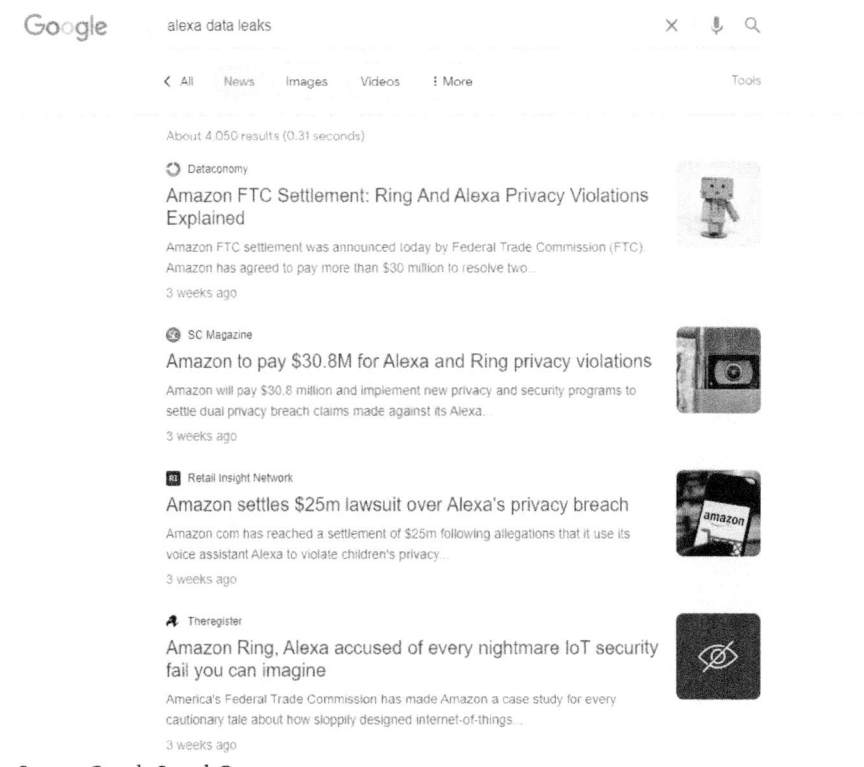

Source: Google Search Page.

As the Internet of Things network of hardware and software continues to build and grow around us, along with increasingly sophisticated technology, smart speakers' actual application and value will become more real. For example, a smart speaker connected to a smart fridge connected to a wider real-world supply chain and a wider pool of customer data can finally mean you're never out of milk, and what could start with 'Hey Alexa, order milk', could eventually lead us to forget Alexa is even there. The out-of-milk scenario is a tired example of the potential of this technology. I love it, and I think it's ironic that we're back to square one.

When Alexa becomes just a cute name for AI software built into several appliances, the smart thermostat or even just the home itself, that knows to order milk even if you forget to ask it; when you ticked a box that said, 'Yes, I'm interested in predictive ordering', and it all just works, then this technology will have arrived.

As far back as 2013, Amazon took out a patent on predictive ordering technology that will be able to order products you want before you've purchased them yourself. Yeah, that's right. Their predictive AI is becoming so advanced that they know what consumers want to buy before they do.

11.4 – PREDICTION 3 – ANTICIPATION BECOMES REAL

(12) United States Patent
Spiegel et al.

(10) Patent No.: US 8,615,473 B2
(45) Date of Patent: Dec. 24, 2013

(54) METHOD AND SYSTEM FOR ANTICIPATORY PACKAGE SHIPPING

(75) Inventors: Joel R. Spiegel, Woodinville, WA (US); Michael T. McKenna, Bellevue, WA (US); Girish S. Lakshman, Issaquah, WA (US); Paul G. Nordstrom, Seattle, WA (US)

(73) Assignee: Amazon Technologies, Inc., Reno, NV (US)

(*) Notice: Subject to any disclaimer, the term of this patent is extended or adjusted under 35 U.S.C. 154(b) by 0 days.

(21) Appl. No.: 13/594,195

(22) Filed: Aug. 24, 2012

(65) Prior Publication Data
US 2012/0323645 A1 Dec. 20, 2012

Related U.S. Application Data

(62) Division of application No. 13/305,611, filed on Nov. 28, 2011, now Pat. No. 8,271,398, which is a division of application No. 11/015,288, filed on Dec. 17, 2004, now Pat. No. 8,086,546.

(51) Int. Cl.
G06Q 99/00 (2006.01)

(52) U.S. Cl.
USPC 705/332; 705/330; 705/333; 705/336; 705/337

(58) Field of Classification Search
USPC 705/332, 330, 333, 336, 337
See application file for complete search history.

(56) **References Cited**

U.S. PATENT DOCUMENTS

6,055,520 A	4/2000	Heiden et al.
6,394,354 B1	5/2002	Wilz et al.
6,827,273 B2	12/2004	Wilz et al.
6,994,253 B2	2/2006	Miller et al.
7,006,989 B2	2/2006	Bezos et al.
7,130,803 B1	10/2006	Couch et al.
7,222,081 B1	5/2007	Sone
7,610,224 B2	10/2009	Spiegel
7,664,653 B2	2/2010	Dearing
8,086,546 B2	12/2011	Spiegel et al.
2001/0037316 A1	11/2001	Shiloh

(Continued)

FOREIGN PATENT DOCUMENTS

JP 2002109263 4/2002
JP 2003067645 3/2003

(Continued)

OTHER PUBLICATIONS

Office Action from Application No. 2007-546877, mailed Apr. 26, 2011, Amazon Technologies, Inc., 8 pages.

(Continued)

Primary Examiner — Akiba Allen
(74) Attorney, Agent, or Firm — Robert C. Kowert; Meyertons, Hood, Kivlin, Kowert & Goetzel, P.C.

(57) **ABSTRACT**

A method and system for anticipatory package shipping are disclosed. According to one embodiment, a method may include packaging one or more items as a package for eventual shipment to a delivery address, selecting a destination geographical area to which to ship the package, shipping the package to the destination geographical area without completely specifying the delivery address at time of shipment, and while the package is in transit, completely specifying the delivery address for the package.

24 Claims, 11 Drawing Sheets

Source: US Patent Office.

This technology, referred to as 'anticipatory shipping', utilises Amazon's extensive customer data to predict consumer preferences in advance. Items that are expected to be in demand are then shipped to a central hub to expedite delivery when the order is placed.

By employing this system, Amazon aims to enhance the customer experience by providing faster delivery times, which could lead to increased repeat business. Additionally, automating the ordering process helps to streamline operations for Amazon and reduce the workload for their employees.

Whereas 'Hey Alexa' requires a request, anticipatory purchasing could use data points, from conversations in the home to the prompt or order regularly used. The next milk bottle could arrive on the day the last is finished without a conscious human purchase involved. Consumers may risk giving up their privacy for this kind of value exchange, especially if everyone is doing it, or it could save their life.

Imagine hearing your friend rave about how an ambulance appeared at their doorstep 20 minutes before their elderly mother had a life-threatening stroke. Alexa detected changes in her voice patterns, modelled those patterns, and determined a high chance of cognitive impairment and a likely emergency. Don't you love your mother enough to pay £50, £10 per month, and possibly waive some of her personal privacy if it means never worrying about finding her unresponsive at the bottom of the stairs? That's more than enough to tip the value for most.

11.5 – PREDICTION 4 – MORE MONEY FOR LAWYERS

There will be continued legal disputes over data sovereignty on both national and local levels. We will also see more legal wrangling (and hopefully fair legislation) around the political and ethical conditions of allowing greater data-fuelled personalisation in specific services, such as health insurance.

Our recent example and Cannes winner Data Tienda shows us the good that better data can do in people's lives. Thousands of people got access to finance because banks were able to use previously unused data to provide them with a credit score. Of course, the emphasis is on those winners that got a usable credit score, but what about those that got a bad credit score? Arguably nothing has changed; they couldn't get credit before and still can't, but what happens when we start applying better data to established markets, such as health insurance?

In countries like America, where giant corporations privatise healthcare, could and should better data be used to deny people health insurance and healthcare? This certainly could be an area where people previously granted health insurance could have that insurance taken away or increased heavily in price, quickly and without any safety nets to cushion their fall.

Companies already offer seemingly innocent perks to those willing to share their personal fitness data through FitBit.

They are ready to prove they can tick off certain fitness and healthy living goals like regular walks. The use of that data is currently relatively benign and overall positive. Still, there are over 20 clinical trials in the USA alone using Fitbits. With time, researchers and doctors will get even better at identifying signals of specific diseases in wearable devices' data.

Wearing a fitness tracking device could earn you serious discounts from your health insurance company, which at first, sounds great for the people who participate and good for the companies who want healthier insurance customers.

Like our stroke example, better preventative healthcare could save millions of lives. Many flu treatments work best when administered within 24 hours of the onset of symptoms. But where it's difficult to identify the flu so quickly, a Fitbit could make that much easier. If the device measures a sudden decrease in the number of steps the person takes per day, plus perhaps an elevated resting heart rate or new tremors signalling chills, that could signal the presence of a virus.

If an insurance company has access to that data, it could send a message to the patient. If the person was feeling poorly (rather than just having decided to watch TV all day), they could be encouraged to go to their doctor or an urgent care clinic. The person could see a health professional quickly, get an effective treatment, and be treated pre-emptively before the worst symptoms appear.

So, what is the cause for concern, and why might we need more money for lawyers and lawmakers? This development would have enormous consequences, and the age-old truism that technology is a double-edged sword could not be more applicable here. According to the Centres for Medicare and Medicaid Services, as many as half of all Americans have some condition that could be used to exclude them from coverage, such as cancer, diabetes, or asthma.

In the USA, the health insurance industry wields a massive

amount of financial power, making them a gatekeeper for whether or not someone can afford to get well. With their ability to determine the cost of treatment, these companies can be the difference between a financial setback and utter ruin.

Would people feel able to object if insurance companies required customers to wear fitness trackers or other monitoring devices? What if this was no longer an optional perk? Would new patients provide access to past data a Fitbit collected? Could an insurance company consider it fraud if a user stopped wearing the device or somehow tried to falsify the data?

If used – and regulated – well, these devices can help individual patients change their daily habits to become healthier, saving insurance companies money and passing some of those savings along to customers. Alternatively, the devices could justify denying coverage to the inactive or unhealthy or boosting their insurance rates.

Just because you're wearing a fitness tracker and sharing your data with your insurance company doesn't mean they'll use it to improve your health. With the potential for huge financial gains or losses at stake, insurers will be tempted to use your data in ways that benefit their bottom line more than your well-being. And with the uncertain legal terrain surrounding pre-existing conditions, it's crucial to carefully consider the potential consequences before we all sign up.

Either way, the courts and legislators will continue to battle on, wading through the murkiness of new technology and how it affects our social conventions and attitudes to these coming changes. One thing is clear from the recent lawsuits that are already in progress: it could be very expensive to accidentally find yourself on the wrong side of these ongoing debates.

11.6 – PREDICTION 5 – TECH WRECK REFOCUS

There will be more layoffs, less investment in R&D, and a focus on ROI. This will result in a refocus on business outcomes that, in turn, will encourage SaaS product developers to continue to develop their tools' unique selling points through continued specialisation, modularisation, and integration.

The dot-com bubble (or dot-com boom) was a stock market bubble in the late 1990s. The period coincided with massive growth in internet adoption, a proliferation of available venture capital, and the rapid growth of valuations in new dot-com startups.

During the dot-com crash, many online shopping companies failed and shut down, notably Pets.com, Webvan, and Boo.com, along with several communication companies, such as Worldcom, NorthPoint Communications, and Global Crossing. Others, like Lastminute.com, MP3.com and PeopleSound, survived the burst but were acquired. Larger companies like Amazon and Cisco Systems lost significant portions of their market capitalisation, with Cisco losing 80% of its stock value.

More recently, billions of dollars in value were wiped off major technology stocks like Meta (the owner of Facebook), Alphabet (Google), Netflix, and Amazon last week as investors punished companies for failing to meet expectations.

But that doesn't mean we are headed for another tech wreck as experienced in the early 2000s, says Stake's Eliot Hastie.

'I think it's different. There's a lot of talk about it. You've got all these different signals flashing across the market. But is it at the bottom? Is it a crash? I'm not quite sure because people are still using technology to do things. They're still shopping on Amazon, we're still watching Netflix, we're still buying Apple and interacting with Microsoft software.'

Shares in technology companies rose strongly in 2020 and 2021, buoyed by people forced to work from home under the COVID-19 pandemic conditions. Hastie said the Nasdaq 100, which comprises the biggest technology stocks in the USA, rose 700 per cent during the pandemic. However, post-pandemic, it's now becoming clear that predictions on this growth's sustainability were over-exaggerated, and many of these tech companies appear to have over-resourced in the wake of slumping profits.

In 2023, layoffs have yet again cost tens of thousands of tech workers their jobs; this time, the workforce reductions have been driven by the biggest names in tech, like Google, Amazon, Microsoft, Yahoo, and Zoom. Startups, too, have announced cuts across all sectors, from crypto to enterprise SaaS.

The reasoning behind these workforce reductions follows a familiar script, citing the macroeconomic environment and a need to find discipline on a tumultuous path to profitability. Still, tracking the layoffs helps us understand the impact on innovation, which companies are facing tough pressures, and who is available to hire for the businesses lucky to be growing. It also, unfortunately, serves as a reminder of the human impact of layoffs and how risk profiles may be changing from here.

One of the most alarming stories is from Sam Bankman-Fried, former CEO of now-defunct FTX.

Until recently, Sam Bankman-Fried, or SBF, was crypto's golden boy, known for building his cryptocurrency exchange, FTX, into a $32 billion giant in just two years.

Shortly before the downfall, Sam Bankman-Fried consented openly and now, in hindsight, over confidently to an eye-opening interview where he openly described Crypto as a Ponzi Scheme, essentially claiming the value of anything is what people will pay for it, whether or not it works or could ever work.

Source: Coffeezilla – YouTube Video.

Startups can use exchanges like this to trade real money for tokens or coins, and these tokens or coins can represent real-world rewards for investing in those companies, an alternative to traditional stocks and shares. With companies and CEOs like this enabling the investment of 'just a box' startups, investors may also have invested, and this also helps to explain why investors now may be feeling pragmatic rather than looking to ride the coattails of anything that looks like the next PayPal or Google, instead hoping for some actual returns.

That's going to affect our MarTech Stacks and our data, but hopefully, we'll see companies look to refocus on their core offerings rather than greedily eating into each other's tech stack pies. It is also likely to mean less investment into custom projects and a subscription to technology that can be cut if budgets require it. Companies do remove whole departments if they need to. This can make choosing the wrong tool extremely expensive. In the early 2000s, when WordPress reigned king, there was also Adobe Business Catalyst, which had spent over 10 years building a customer base. Business Catalyst was a hosted (SaaS) all-in-one solution for building and managing business websites, but in 2019 it announced its abrupt closure.

'Adobe is committed to delivering exceptional software and services to our customers. It's in our nature to innovate and try new things, and it was in this spirit we acquired Business Catalyst in 2009. As we refocus on products that broadly provide our customers with the most value, Adobe is announcing the end of development for Business Catalyst as of March 26th, 2018. New sites will no longer be available for purchase starting on June 18th, 2018.

'Adobe will stop hosting existing sites on Business Catalyst on March 26th, 2020. Adobe encourages customers to download their data and migrate to other systems well before March 26th, 2020.'

As the name is coined, Tech Wreck could come in many different forms. It is now more important than ever to truly assess the tech companies we choose to pair with and how much we recommend investing our time and money in them.

◆ ◆ ◆

After reading this chapter, you can make your predictions about where you think things are heading.

Do we need to watch our Fitbits nervously? Will Amazon deliver our milk, or should we have just stuck with the local milkman?

What can we do as marketers and customers to encourage the kind of future we want to be part of?

Next, we'll look at bringing this all to a firm conclusion as we review, and look to break, **The Circle of F**ked Data.**

References And Bibliography

1. TechCrunch. (2023). Tech Industry Layoffs. Retrieved from https://techcrunch.com/2023/02/16/tech-industry-layoffs/
2. Continuous Disclosure: Are we witnessing another tech wreck? (2022). New Zealand Herald. Retrieved from https://www.nzherald.co.nz/business/continuous-disclosure-are-we-witnessing-another-tech-wreck/KF7VJZ4KMFKZ7MVRFJPHL7B7MA/
3. Wikipedia contributors. (2022). Dot-com bubble. In Wikipedia, The Free Encyclopedia. Retrieved from https://en.wikipedia.org/wiki/Dot-com_bubble
4. Hawke, A. (n.d.). Predictive Analytics in Marketing. Hawke Media. Retrieved from https://hawke.ai/blog/predictive-analytics-in-marketing/
5. Effie Worldwide. (2019). Automated Content Creation Using AI [Case study]. Retrieved from https://www.effie.org/case_database/case/HK_2019_E-70-912
6. Vincent, J. (2021). WhatsApp tries again to explain what data it shares with Facebook — and why. ZDNet. Retrieved from https://www.zdnet.com/article/whatsapp-tries-again-to-explain-what-data-it-shares-with-facebook-and-why/
7. Heater, B. (2019). Fitbit Inspire is a fitness tracker for the rest of us. TechCrunch. Retrieved from https://techcrunch.com/2019/02/09/fitbit-inspire/
8. Wigglesworth, R. (2019). Could your Fitbit data be used to deny you health insurance? GovTech. Retrieved from https://www.govtech.com/health/could-your-fitbit-data-be-used-to-deny-you-health-

insurance.html
9. The Guardian. (2023). Geoffrey Hinton, 'godfather of AI', quits Google, and warns dangers of machine learning. Retrieved from https://www.theguardian.com/technology/2023/may/02/geoffrey-hinton-godfather-of-ai-quits-google-warns-dangers-of-machine-learning
10. A comprehensive list of 2023 tech layoffs | TechCrunch. https://techcrunch.com/2023/05/09/tech-industry-layoffs/

CHAPTER 12 – CONCLUSION

In this final pivotal chapter, we confront marketers' ongoing challenges with their data and explore the root causes behind these persistent issues. We shed light on the lack of investment and understanding that continues to plague the industry, hampering progress.

We explore the intriguing impact of Google offering free access to its analytics platform, questioning how it may have inadvertently diminished the perceived value of analytics as a whole. We consider again the future and **what lies ahead for Google and other major tech platforms that shape our digital landscape.**

We untangle the complexities of the data dilemma, revealing valuable insights and paving the way for a brighter future. It's time to break free from **The Circle of F**ked Data** and forge a new path towards data-driven success.

12.1 – THE RINSE AND REPEAT OF F**KED DATA

After reading all this, are you any closer to understanding why your data is F**ked and how to fix it? I hope you now have a much more solid grasp on what digital analytics could be for marketers and developers alike, the challenges we face, and how to overcome those challenges.

Circle of F**KED Data

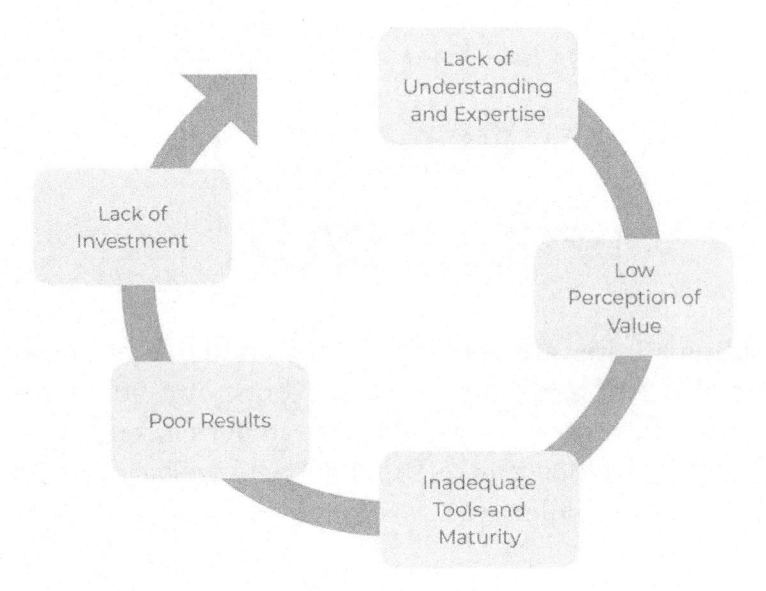

- Lack of Understanding and Expertise
- Low Perception of Value
- Inadequate Tools and Maturity
- Poor Results
- Lack of Investment

Source: Mcktui Consulting.

But it all starts with a need for more understanding, a perception of value, and a motivation or support to care past the short-term goals of individual campaigns. We've divided our people into silos and demarcated business departments without building in the processes, governance, and leadership to ensure we're working towards the Power of One: one voice across all our touchpoints; one shared vision and goal. Then we fill that gap with continued channel-led thinking and a lack of prioritisation for technical foundations and analytics.

1. Lack of **understanding** from all levels of seniority, both overworked marketers with many hats and busy senior stakeholders with more traditional priorities.
2. A **low perception of value** from free and cheap tools, lack of senior stakeholder encouragement, and lack

of proven results. Analytics is generally seen as a necessary enabler to other, more pressing functions.
3. **Inadequate tools and KSAs,** which drive lower levels of analytics maturity due to the lack of interest and investment.
4. Poor data, lack of progress up the Analytics Maturity Curve, and **poor or unprovable results**.
5. **Lack of investment** due to a low perception of value.

How often have you been on a project where a website or campaign goes live without adequate tracking or an agreed framework for success? Our data is flawed to start with, but our problems often begin with making complicated dashboards for the wrong people and not allowing the right people to find gold; the budget goes to quick-fix tools or spending more on campaigns rather than to support proper maintenance of existing tools and tracking.

This is hard stuff for most, but it's completely doable; more often than that, it's repetitive work that people don't want to do or be responsible for because it hasn't been valued or championed within the organisation. A measurement plan can be painful and time-consuming unless you love big spreadsheets, but there is no good way around it. I know – I've tried. If you're not planning what you are tracking and following a detailed naming convention, then you're doing the same work sorting through what came out in reports and which event name matches which button. We could try to get AI to do the heavy lifting, but we still need a human to understand data we are collecting data on our customers and why.

Analytics has, for a long time, been undervalued. It's either a different hat given to the already overburdened jack-of-all-trade marketers or a task given to a Performance Marketer or developer. The Performance Marketer sees it as a way to prove value and will just be concerned with tracking their campaigns; this is often true with agencies. Tracking and reporting regularly breaks as it isn't maintained. Fixing broken tracking is often a game of whack-a-mole, only fixing the things that negatively affect reporting or the current campaign.

Client brands often see analytics as a responsibility of the agency – the agency needs it to tell them, the client, whether the agency is performing. An agency would rarely explain how they didn't hit their KPIs and underdelivered. Really the client should have the confidence to make that decision by owning the analytics piece themselves. But how did this situation come about? In one word – Google. Google's contribution to digital analytics can't be overstated. They took a fledgling company 'Urchin' and reworked the product to the Google Analytics that we know today, that's on nearly every website out there, but they didn't stop there; they offered this fantastic tool to anyone who wanted to use it at no financial cost. They expanded this amazing product with Google Tag Manager, giving more access and power to marketers and an interface to go around developers. Then they created Data Studio, a plug-and-play dashboarding tool so anyone can build dashboards and reports.

The ease of access to these powerful industry-changing tools is undervalued. Still, it is no surprise that Google completely subsidises the tools because this motivates marketers to use other highly profitable ad-purchasing tools, such as Double Click and AdWords. Google's top revenue source in 2022 was search ads. Of the $279.81 billion in revenue the company brought in, a whopping $162.45 billion came from search ads.

A possible indication of the actual retail value of Google Analytics is Google Analytics 360. Especially now, given the development of GA4 and its native connection to BigQuery, there are not many additional features in GA 360 beyond the free version – so much so that even big companies will go to great lengths to avoid paying the cost of upgrading. So why upgrade? Often you may be forced to. The key additional features are Roll-Up Reporting, Custom Funnels, Unsampled Reports, and Custom Tables. But the main reason is removing the deliberate handbrake of Sample Reports. With the paid Google Analytics version, your report is free from sampling if it has less than 100 million sessions. The cost of Google Analytics 360 starts at $150,000 (USD) per year and is billed at $12,500 a month. Costs can increase as well based on the size of the website.

They give all this to us: jack-of-all-trades, blog reading, time-poor, self-taught, quick-fix, short-term problem solvers. Maybe I'm just talking about myself. Of course, there will be recurring issues, lack of reliability, and problems with the data. In most other professions, there is some bar to proving competency. The only bar here is success or failure; get some budget and a laptop and give it a go. I've seen marketers go from job to job, leaving a data analytics path of devastation as they go, but ultimately, they talk the talk and can get good short- to medium-term results.

This problem is compounded by the lack of information from tool providers such as Google, providing a suite of tools with very little support. Pretty much anyone can pick up a laptop and run advertising for clients. Ideally, Google wants to see brands run their own accounts without the need for agencies. Google Analytics, for example, is already costly for Google; they maintain the software, research improvements, and store all your data for free, and they only really provide support for the paid version, which, as we know, is a massive leap in price.

Alternatives like Mixpanel ask for a modest subscription, offer more support, and you can more readily contact someone to discuss the product. However, even with subscription models, most SaaS tool providers know that the money is in getting more subscriptions rather than offering consultation or implementations of their tools. So they offer this work to partners; those partners are often not the most specialised but, rather, large enough so that the tool provider does not have to manage too many individual partners. They will also regularly choose and prioritise the partners who are best at selling rather than at delivery. In my experience, the skills test to becoming a partner often comes down to demonstrating that you can pass easy open book exams, have a 'big enough team', and have a provable pipeline. The last point is the most important.

As analytics becomes riskier, with evermore potential lawsuits on the horizon, and the market continues to mature, we will see Google back away from tools like Google Analytics and move into spaces like Google Cloud. Google Cloud was responsible for $26.28 billion, around 9.4% of the company's 2022 revenues. They built the road, but they'll be happy to have someone come and offer alternatives.

The way forward for companies of all sizes and us marketers is to ensure that a base level of analytics is built into everything we do, with responsibilities, processes, and governance baked into every activity. It is, of course, good to have analytics accountable to one person or team. However, it should be everyone's responsibility to ensure that our data doesn't get F**ked. We can't have contractors working without good documentation of how and why our implementations are in place in case these people leave the company or have cut corners, as we'll continue to see companies cycle through levels 1–3, depending on the in-house skills. We can't assume those using the data will understand it without the libraries to set out what we are looking at.

Digital analytics must be viewed as a long-term, always-on investment; we seek to maintain and build steadily on continuous improvement without heavy reliance on one tool, supplier, or person. This is achieved through deliberate and planned bouts of project-based, plan-led investment to continue to develop our capabilities and service our customers and, critically, stay caught up.

These bouts and cycles of investment must be backed fanatically by at least one senior stakeholder. All investment decisions should be reviewed and approved by all relevant stakeholders, and the decisions should be documented to ensure accountability and transparency. The investment decisions should be aligned with the business's overall strategic goals and unique selling proposition and should also support the strategies of different departments within the company.

There needs to be clear contextual prioritisation of tasks leading to good data, with technical foundation and analytics investment chosen ahead of those seemingly more glamorous items further up the stack, like content and paid, earned, and owned media.

All this is needed to break the cycle of bad data – not just now but for as long as the company is in operation. There is often a considerable reluctance to commit to any long-term project because of the potential risk of it not being completed on time or not fulfilling its objective, but this is not a problem that will be solved overnight, and the issues are systemic. It is not simply a question of whether we should invest heavily in a CRM system, a CDP, or Adobe Analytics, or bite the bullet and invest in 360 or Double Click. By seeing this as a journey and working methodically through the Analytics Maturity Curve to maintain our progress, we can work in short sections to chip away at our end goal.

Chapter 11 looked at the future and the exciting developments that could be coming to us as customers or marketers of those services. One thing rings the loudest to me: those who look after their customers and their data stand the best chance of being left standing. First-party data strategies and omni-channel marketing and personalisation were used to win awards. They were exciting projects as part of our usual digital activities, most of which relied heavily on third-party data. Now, we need to do that which seemed too expensive to do the first time around. We need to focus on really knowing our customers, driving true wisdom, building up our audiences as part of our USP and investing our strategies around owned and earned rather than the short-term wins delivered from a paid performance-led marketing strategy.

This book covers much more than the title suggests. Of course it does, and like you, I'm a marketer first and foremost, and I know the value of a good hook. F**ked data is all of our faults, and there is often not just one simple fix. Still, I hope at least that there are some actionable tools, frameworks, and memorable anecdotes to see you through and make an actionable difference. In every chapter, you will be able to find someone who knows more than me and is more of an expert on that subject than I am. Still, it's been my unique experience and joy to learn from these people who put it all together for my simple mind and then package it again in an understandable, memorable, and approachable way, offering real value.

In conclusion, digital analytics has come a long way in recent years but still faces significant challenges. The siloed nature of our organisations, lack of investment and understanding, and poor data quality all contribute to the current state of affairs. However, with the right mindset and approach, we can overcome these challenges and harness the power of analytics to drive business success. By taking a data-driven approach, working collaboratively across teams and departments, and prioritising foundational technical capabilities and governance, we can unlock insights that help us better understand our customers, make more informed decisions, and drive growth. It's up to us to seize the opportunity and make analytics a truly strategic advantage for our organisations.

There are a lot of 'experts' with their data and analytics, web development, and data science who like to make others feel stupid. Don't let them. Keep asking stupid questions. After all, as Einstein famously said, 'If you can't explain something simply, you don't understand it well enough', and really... who is going to argue with Einstein? Remember that the next time someone instructs you on the complicated reasons why something can't be done.

> "If you can't explain it simply, you don't understand it well enough.."
>
> —Albert Einstein

◆ ◆ ◆

Thank you so much for reading. Good news, I have much more for you on the way. For additional resources and templates, **go to mcktui.com/book**.

GLOSSARY

1. 4P's: Marketing concept comprising product, price, promotion, and place.
2. Above the Line: Advertising approach that targets a mass audience through traditional media.
3. Property (Google Analytics): 'Property' in Google Analytics refers to a website, mobile app, or other digital asset that collects data for analysis. It may say UA:1234556.
4. Action Card: A document or tool outlining a specific action to be taken to achieve a goal. In this case, a personalisation strategy.
5. Agile: Methodology for project management emphasising flexibility and continuous improvement.
6. AIDA: Marketing acronym that stands for Attention, Interest, Desire, Action.
7. Analytics Development Cycle: Framework used to create, test, and deploy data-driven processes.
8. Analytics Maturity Curve: A model that assesses an organisation's analytics capabilities.
9. Application: A software program designed to perform a specific task or set of tasks. In this case, we refer to websites and apps generally as applications or web assets.
10. Artificial intelligence (AI): The simulation of human intelligence by machines.
11. Below the Line: Advertising approach targeting a specific audience through non-traditional media, such as digital marketing.
12. Big Data: Term used to describe extremely large datasets that cannot be processed by traditional data management tools.
13. Blackhat (SEO): Unethical techniques to manipulate search engine rankings, like hidden text, keyword stuffing, and link schemes, violating search engines' terms of service.
14. Bot: An automated software program that performs a specific task, often for a chat or social media. Often seen to inflate sessions and page counts in web analytics tools.
15. Bounce Rate: The percentage of website visitors who leave without navigating to other pages.
16. CDP: Customer Data Platform, a tool used to collect and manage customer data.
17. CEO: Chief Executive Officer, the highest-ranking officer in a company or organisation.

GLOSSARY

18. Channel: A medium or platform used to communicate a message to a target audience.
19. ChatGPT: A conversational artificial intelligence system capable of generating human-like responses.
20. Circle of F**ked Data: A term used to describe the cycle of poor data quality leading to poor decisions and more poor data quality.
21. CJM: Customer Journey Mapping, a process of creating a visual representation of the customer's journey.
22. Client Side: Refers to software that runs on the client or user's computer or device.
23. CMS: Content Management System, a software application for creating and managing digital content.
24. CLV: Customer Lifetime Value, the predicted net profit attributed to the entire future relationship with a customer.
25. CMO: Chief Marketing Officer responsible for developing and executing an organisation's marketing strategy.
26. Code Library: A collection of reusable code for developers to use in their projects.
27. Communication Plan: A document outlining the strategy for communicating with stakeholders in a project or organisation.
28. Content: Information that is intended to be communicated to an audience. Part of the Marketing Stack. This would usually be on a website or other web asset or application.
29. Conversion Rate: The percentage of visitors to a website who complete a desired action.
30. Cookie and Cookie ID: A small data file stored on a user's computer that contains information about their browsing activity on a website.
31. Corporate: Relating to a corporation or large business organisation. Smaller than an Enterprise.
32. CRM: Customer Relationship Management, a strategy for managing a company's interactions with customers and potential customers.
33. CRO: Conversion Rate Optimisation, the process of improving the conversion rate on a website or landing page.
34. C-Suite: Refers to the highest-ranking executives in a company, such as the CEO, CFO, and COO.
35. CTA: Call to Action, a prompt to encourage a user to take a specific action.
36. Customer Attributes: Characteristics or attributes used to describe a customer, such as demographics, interests, and behaviours. Used to build an Audience.
37. Customer Data Platform: A tool used to collect and manage customer data, such as Segments.
38. Customer Journey: The series of interactions a customer has with a company from discovery to post-purchase.
39. Customer Touchpoint: Any point of contact between a customer and a company, such as a website, phone call, or email.

40. Corporate Social Responsibility (CSR): A business model that seeks to balance economic profitability with social and environmental responsibility.
41. Dashboard: A visual representation of data and key performance indicators that provide an at-a-glance view of business performance.
42. Data Integrity: The accuracy, completeness, and consistency of data over its entire lifecycle.
43. Data Lake: A large repository of raw, unstructured and/or structured data that can be used for advanced analytics and machine learning.
44. DMP: Data Management Platform, a tool used to collect, organise, and analyse data for marketing purposes, such as DoubleClick.
45. Data Mining: The process of analysing large data sets to discover patterns, relationships, and insights.
46. Data Policy: A set of guidelines and rules for managing data within an organisation or system.
47. Data P's or Data Management Lifecycle: The various stages of managing data, including data provenance (tracking the origin of data), data privacy (ensuring legal use), data protection (ensuring security and availability), and data preparation (transforming data into insights).
48. Data Resource: Any data or information that is collected, stored, and managed as an asset to support business operations, analysis, and decision-making.
49. Data Sovereignty: The idea that data is subject to the laws and governance of the country in which it is located or originated.
50. Data Strategy: A plan for managing and leveraging data to achieve business objectives and create value.
51. Data Stream (Google Analytics 4): A continuous flow of event data from various sources, such as websites and apps, to Google Analytics 4 for real-time analysis. Now at the Property Level (GA3).
52. Data Warehouse: A centralised repository of data used for reporting and analysis, such as Redshift, Big Query, or Snowflake.
53. DataLayer OR Data Layer: A structured data model used to capture and store data from a website or application.
54. Descriptive Analytics: The use of data to describe past events, such as sales figures, customer behaviour, or website traffic.
55. Developer or Web Developer: A person who writes code and builds applications for the web.
56. DIKW pyramid: A framework that represents the hierarchy of data, information, knowledge, and wisdom.
57. Dimensions and Metrics, Custom or Library Custom Metric and Dimension Library: In web analytics, dimensions are attributes of website visitors, while metrics are measurements of visitor behaviour. It's good practice to organise these in a library.
58. Earned: In digital marketing, earned media refers to publicity gained through promotional efforts other than paid advertising.

GLOSSARY

59. Enterprise: Refers to a large organisation or business.
60. Event, Label, and Action: In web analytics, an event is a specific user interaction with a website, the label is a descriptor of the event, and the action is the resulting behaviour or outcome.
61. Executive Sponsor: A senior leader within an organisation who advocates for and provides resources to support a project or initiative.
62. Federated ID: A method of authentication that allows users to access multiple applications or systems with a single set of login credentials.
63. Fields & Clicks: Refers to the data captured by a web analytics tool, including fields such as page views, clicks, and conversions.
64. FIM: File Integrity Monitoring, a cybersecurity technique that detects changes to files and systems that may indicate a security breach.
65. Fingerprinting: A tracking technique that identifies individual devices or users based on unique characteristics such as browser settings, installed fonts, or screen resolution.
66. First, Second, and Third Party: Refers to different sources of data in digital marketing; first-party data comes from the business's own website or application, second-party data comes from a partner or affiliate, and third-party data comes from an external source.
67. FTX: A cryptocurrency exchange platform that allows users to trade and invest in various cryptocurrencies and digital assets.
68. GA 360: Google Analytics 360, a premium version of Google Analytics with additional features and support.
69. GAP Analytics Team: A team responsible for identifying gaps in business processes and data collection and proposing solutions to improve business performance.
70. GDPR: EU data protection law safeguarding privacy rights and empowering individuals with control over their personal information. General Data Protection Regulation.
71. Go: A strategy board game for two players, originating from China. The game is played on a grid of black lines, and the objective is to surround more territory than the opponent.
72. Google Analytics or GA3/GA4: A web analytics tool provided by Google that tracks and reports website traffic and user behaviour.
73. Google Cloud: A cloud computing platform and infrastructure offered by Google.
74. Google Debugger: A tool used to troubleshoot and debug issues with Google Analytics tracking code.
75. Growth: as featured in the Pillars to Personalisation. The ultimate goal of the pillars is to personation as part of Growth Marketing generally.
76. GTM: Google Tag Manager, a tool used to manage and deploy marketing and analytics tags on a website.
77. Hard Skills: Specific technical or job-related skills that are

necessary for performing a particular job or task.
78. HIPPO: Highest-Paid Person's Opinion, a situation where the opinion of a senior executive carries more weight than other data or input.
79. iFrames: An HTML element used to embed content from one website into another website. Difficult to track as it's seen as being on two separate pages at the same time.
80. Incognito Browser and Cloak: A browsing mode that does not save browsing history or cookies, used to browse the web anonymously. A cloak is a technique used to hide or disguise a website's true identity or location.
81. Infrastructure as featured in the Marketing Stack: The underlying technology, hardware, and software used to support marketing initiatives and data collection.
81. Internet of Things (IoT): The interconnectivity of everyday devices and appliances through the internet.
82. Information Technology (IT): The use of computers, software, and telecommunications equipment to process, store, retrieve, and transmit data.
83. IT People Lock-in: The phenomenon of IT employees developing a deep knowledge of a particular technology or system and becoming resistant to change.
84. Key Performance Indicator (KPI): A measurable value that demonstrates how effectively a company is achieving its key objectives.
85. Knowledge, Skills, and Abilities (KSA): The set of attributes required to perform a particular job, including education, experience, and competencies.
86. Landing Pages: A standalone web page designed to capture a visitor's information through a form; often used in marketing campaigns.
87. Lean: A methodology that focuses on creating more value with fewer resources by eliminating waste and streamlining processes.
88. Levels 1–5: A framework used to measure an organisation's data maturity and effectiveness. See Analytics Maturity Curve.
89. Log File: A record of events that occur on a computer or network, used for troubleshooting and analysis.
90. Looker: A business intelligence tool that enables organisations to analyse and visualise their data. Previously Data Studio.
91. Lifetime Value (LTV): The total revenue a customer is expected to generate over the course of their relationship with a company. See Customer Lifetime Value.
92. Machine Learning: A type of artificial intelligence that enables machines to learn from data and improve their performance without being explicitly programmed.
93. Marketing Automation Tool: Software that automates repetitive marketing tasks and workflows, such as email campaigns and lead scoring.

GLOSSARY

94. Marketing Stack: An approach to understanding marketing, technology, and strategy. Created by Ian Lurie.
95. Marketing Website: A website designed to promote a product or service and generate leads or sales.
96. MarTech Stack: The collection of marketing technologies used by a company to manage their marketing operations.
97. Measurement Plan: A document that outlines the metrics and data sources used to measure the effectiveness of a marketing campaign or initiative.
98. Metaverse: A collective virtual shared space created by the convergence of physical and virtual reality. Created by Meta.
99. Modularity: The design principle of breaking a system down into smaller, independent components that can be easily modified or replaced.
101. Multi-cloud Support: The ability to deploy and manage applications across multiple cloud environments.
102. Omni-channel: Seamless integration of all channels to provide a consistent customer experience. The result of proper personalisation.
103. One-Trick Pony: Limited capabilities or focus. Tying the same thing repeatedly and expecting it to work.
104. Opportunity Cost: The cost of passing up on the next best alternative when making a decision.
105. Owned: Marketing channels that are controlled by the company (e.g. website, social media).
106. Paid: Marketing channels that require payment to use (e.g. advertising).
107. Panda: A Google algorithm update that penalised websites with low-quality content. See Blackhat SEO.
108. Paradigm Shift: A fundamental change in approach or underlying assumptions.
109. Parameters: Values passed to a function or method to customise its behaviour.
110. Pathway to Personalisation: A framework for developing a personalisation strategy.
111. Payment Gateways: Services facilitating online payments (e.g. PayPal, Stripe).
112. Penguin: A Google algorithm update that penalised websites for spammy backlinks.
113. Performance Management: Setting goals, measuring progress, and taking corrective action to improve performance.
114. Personalisation: Tailoring products, services, or experiences to

meet individual customers' specific needs or preferences.
115. Personalisation Strategy Matrix: A tool for mapping personalisation efforts based on their level of complexity and value.
116. PII: Personally Identifiable Information. See GDPR.
117. Pillars of Personalisation: Key components of a successful personalisation strategy (data, technology, content, and testing).
118. Pixel and JavaScript SDK: Tools used for tracking website or app activity.
119. POS: Point of sale.
120. Post Back: A server-to-server communication that sends data from one server to another.
121. Power of One: A philosophy that emphasises the impact of individual action and responsibility.
122. Predictive Analytics: The use of data, statistical algorithms, and machine learning techniques to forecast future outcomes.
123. Prescriptive Analytics: Analysing data to determine the best course of action for a given situation.
124. Product/Application: A software or web application that serves as a customer portal or marketing site.
125. Programmatic: The automated buying and selling of advertising in real-time through a software platform.
126. Project Plan: A detailed outline of tasks, timelines, and resources required to complete a project.
127. Propensity to Convert: A measure of a customer's likelihood to complete a desired action, such as making a purchase.
128. Research and Development (R&D): The process of creating and improving products through scientific and technological research.
129. RACI Matrix: A tool used to define roles and responsibilities for a project or process.
130. Report: A document that presents information in an organised format for a specific audience.
131. Reporting Structure and Strategy: The framework for how data is collected, analysed, and presented to stakeholders.
132. Retargeting: The practice of serving ads to people who have previously interacted with a brand or product.
133. Return on Investment (ROI): A calculation used to determine the profitability of an investment.
134. Risk and Readiness Review (RRR): An evaluation of potential risks and readiness to manage them.
135. Software as a service (SaaS): A software delivery model in which software is hosted and maintained by a vendor and accessed remotely by users.
136. Segmentation: The process of dividing a target market into

GLOSSARY

smaller groups based on common characteristics or behaviours.

137. Self-Service Dashboards: Tools that allow users to create customised reports and visualisations without the need for technical expertise.
138. Search Engine Marketing (SEM): A form of online advertising that promotes websites by increasing their visibility in search engine results pages.
139. Search Engine Optimisation (SEO): The practice of optimising a website's content and structure to increase its visibility and ranking in search engine results pages.
141. Server-Side tracking: A method of collecting user data in the server rather than in the client machine using cookies or pixels.
142. Session: A period of time during which a user interacts with a website or application before logging out.
143. Silo: A situation where different departments or teams within a company work independently and do not communicate or collaborate effectively.
144. Six Sigma: A methodology for process improvement and quality control that aims to eliminate defects and reduce variability.
145. SMART: An acronym for Specific, Measurable, Achievable, Relevant, and Time-bound, used as a framework for setting goals.
146. Smart Tech: Technology that uses artificial intelligence or machine learning to automate tasks or provide personalised experiences.
147. Small or Medium Enterprise or SME: A company with fewer than 250 employees and annual revenue under a certain threshold.
148. Snowflake: A cloud-based data warehousing platform that allows for the storage, processing, and analysis of large amounts of data.
149. Snowplow: An open-source platform for collecting, processing, and modelling event data from websites, mobile apps, and other sources.
150. Social Media Platform (e.g. Facebook, LinkedIn, Twitter): Online platforms that allow users to create and share content, connect with others, and engage with brands and businesses.
151. Soft Skills: Non-technical skills such as communication, teamwork, and problem-solving that are important in the workplace.
152. Solution Design: The process of creating a plan or blueprint for a product or service that meets the needs of the customer or user. Used to organise and design the connections between technologies such as MarTech.
153. Stakeholder: A person or group with an interest or involvement in a project or business.
154. Statistical Modelling: The use of statistical methods to analyse and model data in order to make predictions or decisions.
155. Steering Committee: A group of stakeholders responsible for overseeing and guiding a project or initiative.

156. Strategy Nutshell: A concise summary of a company's overall strategy, goals, and objectives.
157. Tag Management System (e.g. GTM): A system that allows for the management and deployment of a website's or mobile app's tags, scripts, and pixels.
158. Tech Companies: Companies that develop and sell technology products and services, such as hardware, software, and digital platforms.
159. Tech Wreck: A period of economic downturn or market collapse specifically affecting the technology industry.
160. The Divide: A term used to describe the gap or divide between different groups or communities, particularly in relation to access to technology and digital resources.
161. The GAP or Chasm: A concept that describes the difficulty of achieving widespread adoption of an innovation.
162. The Two Tracks: The parallel skill sets within an organisation in relation to marketing and technology.
163. Tier Target Per Asset: Defining the detail of tracking required for a web asset. Tiers 1–3.
164. Touchpoint: Any interaction channel between a customer and a brand, including physical interactions and digital interactions, such as website visits and social media engagement.
165. Track One: Refers to hard skills and emphasis on code and technology.
166. Track Two: Refers to soft skills and emphasis on people and processes.
167. Turnkey Solution: A product or service that is ready to use immediately, without any additional setup or configuration required.
168. Tyre-kickers: A term used to describe potential customers who are not serious about making a purchase but are simply gathering information.
169. URL (Uniform Resource Locator): The web address of a particular webpage or resource on the internet.
170. User Journey Mapping: The process of creating a visual representation of the steps a user takes when interacting with a product or service.
171. UX or User Experience: Refers to the overall experience a user has when interacting with a product or service, including its ease of use, functionality, and design.
172. Value Exchange: Refers to the exchange of value between a business and its customers, where customers receive value in exchange for their time, attention, or money.
173. Variable: A placeholder for a value that can change over time or in different situations, often used in statistical analysis.
174. Vendor Lock-in: A situation in which a customer becomes dependent on a particular vendor for a product or service, making it difficult to switch to a different vendor.
175. Walled Gardens: Refers to closed ecosystems, such as social

media platforms or app stores, where access and content are tightly controlled by the owner.
176. Web Analytics: Tools used to collect, measure, and analyse data on website performance and user behaviour, including Google Analytics, Matomo, Mixpanel, Tealeaf, and Hotjar.
177. Web Assets in Scope: Refers to the websites, applications, and other digital properties that are being evaluated or analysed as part of a project or initiative.
178. Web Tag: A snippet of code that is added to a website or web application to track user behaviour and collect data for web analytics and other digital marketing tools.
179. Wheel of Growth: A framework used to help businesses identify and prioritise growth opportunities and strategies through personalisation.
180. Work in Progress (WIP): Refers to tasks, projects, or initiatives that are currently underway but not yet completed.
181. Wireframe: A visual representation of a website or application that outlines its layout and structure, often used in the design and development process.
182. Working Group: A team of individuals with diverse skills and expertise who collaborate on a specific project or initiative.

ADDITIONAL RESOURCES

Appendix 1 Raci Matrix

Project/ Deliverable*	(PS)	(BA)	(HDA)	(WAS)	(PM)	(MM)	(WD)
Master (All projects)	C	A	C	R	R	I	R
Engagement Tracking – Field Tracking	A	I	A	I	R	C	R
User Tracking – Data Layer	A	I	C	I	I	C	R
Data Checking	A	I	A	R	R	I	R
Reporting and Insights	C	A	A	R	R	C	I
Project and Communication Plan	C	A	A	I	R	C	I
Code Registry and Developer Instructions	A	I	C	C	I	I	R
Solution Design (use and combination	C	A	C	I	I	I	I

of tools)							
Measurement Plan and Checklist	A	I	A	R	R	I	R

*To be confirmed – Example only.

Key:

R	Responsible: means they are involved in completing the task for review
A	Accountable refers to the final approving authority for the task who signs off
C	Consulted reflects the subject matter experts and others consulted on the task
I	Informed indicates those who are kept up to date about the progress

Appendix 2 Key Projects

Projects by Stage and Type of Work	Detail	Target Start *	Estimated Hours
IMPLEMENTATION			
CDP Research/ Integration	Double-check segment suitability	Jan	5 Hours
Consent Management	Segment Integration with a Consent Management tool	Jan	2 Hours
Tracking Implementation	Shoe-in.com. The immediate requirement is defined in the MP	Feb	10 hours (inc. Implementation and testing)
Tracking Implementation	Shoe-in.co.uk. The immediate	Feb	15 hours (inc. Implement

	requirement is defined in the MP		ation and testing)
Tracking Implementation	Shoe-in.design.com. The immediate requirement is defined in the MP	Feb	30 hours (inc. Implementation and testing)
Tracking Implementation	Shoe-in/portal.com. The immediate requirement is defined in the MP	Feb	30 hours (inc. Implementation and testing)
CONNECTIONS			
Segment – Current choice for CDP	Segment connection and integration are required	Mar	2 Hours
BigQuery/ Microsoft Azure SQL Development	Schema design/ development	Mar	5 Hours
REPORTING AND DASHBOARDING			
Strategic Dashboard	Senior level	May	TBC
Tactical Dashboard	Error reports	April	TBC
Tactical Dashboard	Field-level funnel reports	April	TBC
Tactical Dashboard	Page level funnel reports	April	TBC
Dashboard and Report Scoping	Top-level scoping of report structure and progress checks	Mar	April
Ad-hoc insights and reporting	As required	TBC	TBC
MARTECH INTEGRATIONS			
MarTech Integration – Per Asset	Google Ads/ YouTube – source & destination	Mar	Mar
MarTech Integration	Facebook – source &	Mar	Mar

– Per Asset	destination		
MarTech Integration – Per Asset	Salesforce – source & destination	Mar	Mar
Marketing Audiences	Defined in 3rd party tools using CDP data. Support as required	Apr	Apr
BACK-END AND OFFLINE INTEGRATIONS			
Back-End Systems Integration	As required – Connect through segment	June	June
Marketing Data Integration – Offline	In-store POS	June	TBC
PREDICTION AND PERSONALISATION			
Data Science / Personas	Pull insights from the data warehouse back into segment personas via SQL traits	Jul	TBC
TESTING			
Federated ID Cross Check	Cross-check to confirm that it is working for ALL sources and destinations	Jul	TBC
Data Checking (Recurring)	As per new tracking and reports	Feb	Ongoing
TRAINING AND WORKSHOPS			
Report Structure and Strategy	Requirements for reporting output for Measurement Plan, Project Plan	Jan	
Risk and Readiness Review	Cross-siloed workshop on three pillars of personalisation – output for Solution	Jan	

	Design and Project Plan		
GA4	July	Mar	Mar
Segment	July	Mar	Mar
STRATEGY AND COMMUNICATION			
Project and Communication Plan	In progress	Jan	Mar
Measurement Planning	In progress	Jan	Jan
Create Libraries for developers	Custom metric and dimension library. Code library and developer instructions.	Jan	Jan
Solution Design	Create initial Solution Design	Jan	Ongoing
Monthly Meetings	See the communication plan	Jan	Ongoing
Weekly WIP's	See the communication plan	Jan	Ongoing
R&D – Time for new sources and destinations	TBC	Jan	Ongoing

Appendix 3 Communication Plan (As Part Of The Project Plan)

PURPOSE
This communication plan aims to inform stakeholders of the project's progress and successes in a structured way.

Communication Plan Objectives:
- Building trust with our stakeholders.

- Providing guidance and framework for effective communication within and outside the project.
- Providing precise and concise project communication at the right time.
- Involving all necessary stakeholders and maintaining regular contact.
- Having clear communication channels with well-defined roles and responsibilities.
- Promoting openness and transparency.

Delivery Support – Daily/As Required.
- Shoe-in Website Developers.
- Web Analytics Specialist.
- Strategist & Data Insight Specialist.
- Shoe-in Analyst.

Working Group – Weekly
- Shoe-in Website Developers/Product Manager (as requested, dependent on the project stage).
- Shoe-in Marketing Manager.
- Shoe-in Business Analyst.
- Absolute Analytics Web Analytics Specialist.
- Head of Analytics (as requested, see budget).
- Group Marketing Manager (as requested). More time is required initially.

Note that WIPs are recorded for missing attendees or future review of tasks.

Steering Committee – Monthly/Quarterly
- Head of Analytics – Co-leading.
- Shoe-in Executive Project Sponsor.
- Group Marketing Manager.
- Marketing Operations Manager.

The Shoe-in team will be updated via regular emails, video meetings and Asana to ensure transparency and clear communication.

Appendix 4 Example Solution Design – Stages And Phases

Stage	In-scope digital assets	Detail
Phase 1	Web Analytics / Customer Data Platform / TMS	**Data Collection** • Client-side events via tagging of the shoe-in.com marketing websites. Likely use of Google Tag Manager as TMS – depending on whether we use Telium or Segment.
2	Customer Data Platform	**Data Management – Syndicate – Personalisation Strategy** • Implement chosen CDP solution. Integrate with existing servers. • Implementation of the CDP to: ➢ Connect and streamline data flow from sources to destinations. ➢ Govern data privacy policies and streamline GDPR and CCPA compliance. • Pass back-end-generated Federated ID to all Web Applications.
3	CDP / Marketing Systems	**Marketing Data Integration – Online – Personalisation Strategy** • Integrate existing MarTech tools (e.g. Google, Facebook, MailChimp) as sources & destinations.
4	Web Analytics / Data Warehous	**Reports and Dashboarding** • Connection to web analytics (GA4) and data warehouse (BigQuery) for setup of strategic and tactical dashboards.

	e / Reporting Level 3 – Achieved	• Scoping and setup up strategic and tactical dashboards. • Training Plan.
5	Offline/ CDP / Back-End Systems Level 4 – Achieved	**Data Collection – Off and On – Personalisation Strategy** • Additional Server-side events and additional offline and back-end systems (e.g. footfall tracker and POS) ◦ If not applicable, data extraction will be ready for manual loads.
6	CDP / Data Warehouse Level 5 – Achieved	**Analysis – Predictive Analytics – Personalisation Strategy** • Pull insights generated from the data warehouse back into segment personas via SQL traits.

ABOUT THE AUTHOR

Mark Mckenzie

Mark McKenzie, starting his career in media in London, has amassed over a decade of experience in the field of digital marketing and analytics. Throughout his journey, he has collaborated with SMEs, corporates, and enterprises, establishing highly specialised consultancy and agency departments that prioritise digital analytics. Serving clients across New Zealand, the United Kingdom, Australia, and the USA, Mark has encountered and tackled challenging questions from struggling marketers in diverse industries, spanning web analytics tools, platforms, connections, and databases. It is this wealth of real-life experience that forms the foundation of this book.

Your Data is F**ked bridges the gap between the technical realities of digital marketing and the strategic objectives of senior stakeholders. Each theory, idea, and framework presented within has been thoroughly vetted by the brands, marketers, and business owners whom Mark has served and continues to collaborate with. He is not merely an armchair critic or an intellectual researcher but an active participant in the field, working alongside professionals every step of the way.

Following the sale of his consultancy, Mark briefly assumed the role of Head of Analytics in sunny Auckland, ensuring the successful transfer of his specific knowledge and skills. He was also a founding member and Director (Auckland) of the internationally renowned conference 'MeasureCamp' and supported the community by regularly hosting and organising 'Web Analytics Wednesday' events.

While he now resides in the not-so-sunny UK with his family, Mark continues to engage in consulting, sailing, and working on various projects.

For more information go to: www.mcktui.com.

Printed in Great Britain
by Amazon